ROLL AGAIN SECOND ARMORED

The Prelude to Fame 1940-43

By
Maj. Norris H. Perkins (Ret.)
and
Michael E. Rogers

First published 1988

ISBN 0 904811 11 5

Produced and published for the authors by Kris-
tall Productions Ltd, 71b Maple Road, Surbiton,
Surrey, KT6 4AG, England.

Front cover illustration shows the M4A1 Sherman tank 'Hannibal', Company H, 66th Armored
Regiment, 2nd Armored Division, commanded
by Captain Norris H. Perkins during the attack
on Canicatti, Sicily, July 12, 1943.
Painting by Mark Postlethwaite.

Printed and bound by
Adlard and Son Limited,
Dorking, Surrey, and Letchworth, Hertfordshire

This book was developed by:
Major Norris H. Perkins, text and photos (unless stated otherwise).
Michael E. Rogers, sub text, technical data, materiel identification, photo printing, formatting/typsetting/design (using an Apple® Macintosh Plus™ computer, a desk top publishing system), and coordination.

with contributions by:
Master Sgt. Bernard Hylinski, photos and letters
Staff Sgt. John J. Young, photos and letters
Staff Sgt. Arden Gatske, epilog and letters
Staff Sgt. Timothy C. McMahan, photo and letters
Malcolm J. Stalker, photos
Terrill Aitken - Oregon Historical Military Museum, photos
Mike Carlson
Chris Ellis
Dan Graves
Donald E. Houston
Kevin J. Kiedrowski
Betty Perkins
Ian J. Phillips
Gail A. Rogers

For other memories of our greatest fulfilment:
Ralph E. Brill; James M. Burt; Curtis M. Clark; Benjamin F. Crouse Jr.; Thomas M. Domarecki ; Kenneth F. Grogan, Jr.; Hubert E. Gwinn; Paul Hoffman; Cecil Lands; Harry J. Larson; George O. Lincoln, Jr.; Lt. Col. Frank G. Lumpkin, Jr.; John H. Mayo; William "Butch" Page; Oliver Dix Perkins; Guy Qualls; William Lloyd Rape; Judge F. Murland Smith; Lonzie Ray Spivey; Cameron J. Warren.

Drawings
Sgt. 1st Class Robert J. Torsrud. Sgt. Torsrud served with the Second Armored Division Forward, Germany in 1983-85

This book is dedicated to all members, past and present, of the Second Armored Division.

> **Roll, you armor, roll and roll again,**
> **Turn 'em over and we'll go again,**
> **Roll again to Hell and back again,**
> **We'll go, just tell us when.**

N. H. P. '83

Bibliography

Army Lineage Services, Office of the Chief of Military History, U.S. Army, Washington D.C.
Chamberlain, P. and Ellis, C. *British and American Tanks of World War II*. Arco Publishing, Inc., -1975.
Chamberlain, P. and Ellis, C. *M3 Medium (Lee/Grant)*. Profile Publications Limited, 1972.
Ellis, C. and Chamberlain, P. *Light Tanks M1-M5*. Profile Publications Limited, 1972.
Houston, D. E. *Hell on Wheels*. Presidio Press, 1977.
Hunnicut, R. P. *Sherman*. Presidio Press, 1978.
Icks, R. J. *Tanks and Armored Vehicles*. Phillips Andrews Publishing Co., 1945.
Jones, R. E., Rarey, G. H. and Icks, R. J. *The Fighting Tanks 1916-1933*. WE Inc., 1969.
Medium Tanks M4 and M4A1. TM 9-731A, War Department, 1942.
Trahan, E. A. *A History of the Second United States Armored Division*. Albert Love Interprises, -1946.
Weapons and Warfare. Phoebus Publishing Company/BPC Publishing Ltd. 1971/77/78.

About The Authors

Norris Perkins was commissioned as an Army Reserve Officer in 1935 when he was studying for his degree in architecture at the University of Oregon. He was an expert rifleman and competed in cross country track. After college he was rejected for Flying Cadet with the Army Air Corps because his blood pressure was too high with excitement. In disgust, he immediately took his first private flying lesson. Later, working as an industrial engineer, his hobbies were writing, photography, and private flying.

When Hitler invaded Holland in 1940, 1st Lt. Perkins began his 5 1/2 years of active duty in armor. After two years of intensive training with the Second Armored Division, Capt. Perkins led a tank company in the invasions of North Africa and Sicily. On July 12, 1943 he was wounded in Sicily and received the Distinguished Service Cross and Purple Heart. After seven months in hospitals, during which time he went on speaking tours for the Pentagon, he was appointed Instructor in the Tactics Department of the Armored Force School, at Fort Knox, Kentucky. While teaching officers and officer candidates he rewrote, with two other officers, the basic Field Manuals on tank employment for the Platoon, Company and Battalion, serving as a Major in the last year of the war.

Perkins then took medical training for 11 years and practiced medicine from 1957 to 1986. He never got the Second Armored Division out of his blood and has published several articles and composed two songs about armor.

Michael Rogers is an engineering writer whose hobby has been the writing and publication of many articles on armored vehicles. His military background consists of 4 years in the U.S. Air Force. He was stationed at Vandenburg AFB, Calif. (SAC) and RAF Alconbury, England (TAC) in the mid 1970's. Mike has been the moving force behind this book since he "discovered" Dr. Perkins partly through hearing a tape of his two tank songs. He became excited about Perkins' collection of photos, because of their quality and unusual coverage of men and machines in the field during the intensive training for combat.

Rogers recognized the windfall in this large number of unpublished photos and, in supervising their use, has helped Perkins to somewhat alleviate his feeling of "unfinished business" in the war. There has been so much reportorial writing and photography about combat experiences that it is fortuitous that fate has led Perkins and Rogers to concentrate on an extremely crucial but less publicized period in the history of the Second Armored Division. This book is a real find for armor buffs and the general reader who are bound to be surprised at the amount of action, danger, excitement, inspiration and even a dollop of comedy in the preparation for battle.

Preface

The project of formulating this book really began in 1984. Having gained the reputation of being a "tank nut" with just about everyone I know, I occasionally receive tidbits of armor related information. One such acquaintance, Greg Rekhart, an ex-M60 tanker, called me one evening to let me know his physician was a veteran of the Second Armored Division. Knowing I was heading out on a research trip to Ft. Knox that evening, Greg informed me Dr. Norris H. Perkins hoped I might deliver some information to the Patton Museum for him. I agreed, and that is how the project of writing this book began.

Unfortunately for we military researchers, war veterans usually do not understand our interest or intentions. Norris did not completely fit this picture. He was more than pleased I was interested in his collection of WWII armor manuals but was curious about what I could do with such information. At our first meeting, Norris, with the skill of a doctor, quietly and patiently set about trying to figure out what made this "guy" tick. After realizing my enthusiasm and appreciation for what he had collected, he shyly asked if I might be interested in seeing a photo album of his armor years. He stated; "I doubt if there's anything you'd be interested in. They're just a lot of pictures only old tankers like myself want to look at."

Needless to say, I immediately realized the historical importance of what Norris had had sitting on his library shelves all these years, and suggested to him he share the photos with people who really did appreciate what he had. Now when I look back at that most enjoyable visit with Norris, I still believe he was surprised so many people, other than veteran tankers, could find the subject exciting.

After spending about a year sifting through the photos and gathering information from Norris about each one, and trying to come up with complete and meaningful sub- texts, I came to an impasse. My original concept of a pictorial book gave way to the realization that the photos deserved much more. Being a researcher is one thing, being an ex-tanker is another. Who better to write about the time than Norris? I approached him with the idea of writing the text and he enthusiastically agreed.

In the time that followed, Norris became a fellow researcher, poring over all of the letters he had written home and the lecture notes he had taken at the Armored Force School during the early forties, and phoned or met with his war buddies during Second Armored reunions. While digging through his memorabilia and keepsakes, he found the original negatives which had lain dormant for over forty years, so I began the process of printing them and researching the vehicles which materialized on the paper.

As you will find, Norris has recreated the very fervor of the time and revives the aura and drama of men and machines in the formative years of the mighty Second Armored Division. I hope my efforts have given the reader a faithful look at the materials of war used by them.

Michael E. Rogers
Aloha, Oregon
Summer, 1987

Introduction

If you are not too squeamish, we hope this book will put you in a tank, in spirit, with your crew.

It is not basically about armies, generals, campaigns and battles. It is an intimate look at some of the war machines and the roots of inspired teamwork and growing fame in the pre-war years and the first combat performance of the Second Armored Division. It reveals the sources of a soldier's bonds and how he could have a love affair with a rolling iron coffin. It describes the excitement, danger, accidents and benefits of realistic training, and how some of these experiences were applied in battle.

When Hitler invaded the Lowlands in May, 1940 his panzers were using some of the tactics we had already developed in theory, ideas which German officers visiting the U.S. in the 1930s said they too were developing. They probably were a little behind us in doctrine but ahead of us in vehicle development. We were ahead in a new weapon, the .50 caliber machine gun, which we kept under wraps. The Germans' shocking success in their blitzkriegs precipitated us into forming our Armored Force in June 1940, as hopes for neutrality and isolation were fading.

Many of our pre-existing small tank units, under infantry or cavalry control, stationed in eastern or mid-western states, were transferred to Ft. Knox and Ft. Benning as nuclei for the first two armored divisions. Although our story begins in 1940, several pre-1940 tanks are included in the photos, to give a broader perspective of the evolution of American tanks.

The events and adventures described are as seen through the eyes of a platoon and company grade tank officer.

N.H.P.

Major General George Smith Patton, United States Army, Retired, wrote about this book on January 25, 1988, "....I must say, I truly enjoyed it. ....Again, my hearty congratulations. ....Veteran tanker, Norris Perkins, has effectively recaptured the early activities and operational experiences of that indomitable group of World War II soldiers who manned "Hell on Wheels", the Army's most famous Armored Division."

(General Patton, a much decorated veteran of the Korean and Vietnam wars had a reputation both for toughness and a deep affection for his soldiers. He commanded the Second Armored Division from 1975 to 1977. He operates a commercial farm in Massachusetts and has many other activities, including racing sailing. His father, General George S. Patton Jr., "Ol' Blood and Guts", commanded the same Second Armored in 1940-42.)

Contents

Chapter 1

Chapter 2

Chapter 3

Chapter 4

Chapter 1

Birth of the Second Armored Division

Vaguely at first you hear a hundred giant cog-wheels rolling unclad down an iron road. Then they become a battalion of ancient Trojan chariots, their wheels pounding the stony plain. In the early dawn you wake up to remember that you are at Ft. Benning, Georgia. It is August, 1940. There is an aura of urgency in the frightful racket. You crawl out of your bunk and feel your way to a window. Now the gnashing of steel sprockets blends with the roar of motors. As they pass, you can see a man's head in the cupola of each tank, each wearing a rubber-haloed crash helmet. The faces are serious, cavalry men riding out on a mission. Can it be that this great noise is their way of proclaiming their superiority over the soldiers still asleep in the barracks?

A newcomer could quickly read about Ft. Benning in a brochure sold at the Post Exchange. It covered 97,245 acres of rolling open country and woodland on the Chattahoochee River. 25,000 enlisted men and 1500 officers were permanently stationed there. The post included Lawson Field, an Air Corps base. At that time it was the home of the famous Infantry School; the 4th Division, just becoming completely motorized; numerous separate battalions,

You crawl out of your bunk and feel your way to the window.

A post card of M2A2 light tanks on the attack during maneuvers at Ft. Benning, Georgia.

other units and the **Second Armored Division**, one of the first two divisions in the just-created Armored Force. The First Armored Division was at Ft. Knox, Kentucky.

Little did we know that our assignment, the 2nd Armored Division, would become one of the best trained and most famous of all armored divisions in any army and that we would become the elite, among the best tankers in the world. This is the story of why that came about, the story of the adventures of men and machines as they were fused and fine tuned into the overture of fame and fulfillment.

Above:
America's early experiment with armor, the British designed and U.S. built 44 ton Mark VIII. 100 Mark VIIIs were produced by the Ordnance Department in 1919. Top speed: 6 mph. (Oregon Historical Military Museum)

Right:
U.S. Army Six Ton M 1917 (copy of French Renault) tanks on maneuvers; 952 of these vehicles were produced by the U.S. between 1918 and 1919.
(Oregon Historical Military Museum)

The Machines And The Men

Come ride with us now, dear reader, as we roll again with "Hell on Wheels," and learn of the ardor of armor.

The characteristics of tanks and other armored vehicles were what appealed to us. We learned by doing and were soon initiated into the facts of strategic mobility and surprise; great fire power; maneuverability, as in the old cavalry; shock action (physical and morale effect); armor protection and obstacle ability. The practice of these abilities taught us too the difficulty of concealment because of size and noise, the problems of terrain and the factors of mechanical deterioration and personnel fatigue.

In mid-1940, a number of regional enlistees joined the division which soon completed the ranks with thousands of selectees. Reserve officers came from all over the country.

A fascinating mix of American accents was heard, with the whole spectrum from New England twangs to the various drawls of the deep South, the pioneer cultures from the Central States and those of us from the Far West who thought we had no accent. Conservative New England Damnyankees joined with Southern Rebels in a wonderful exchange of colloquialisms, slang, humor, attitudes and, yes, fights.

Later, when caderies were sent to form other new armored divisions we had to be filled up again with replacements. One day my tank company received 35 "selectees", supposedly selected for their backgrounds and skills. Their

Six Ton M 1917 being loaded onto a T-C-S-W (Tank Carrier Six Wheel). Forty eight of these tank transporters were produced by the Quartermaster Corps in 1929. (Oregon Historical Military Museum)

names all began with J and K! Many were from the Great Lakes region and there were names like Jacoby, Jaeck, Jendrzeyewski, Kaddatz, Kasner, Kubalak and Kunkel. A lot of these men were truck drivers, mechanics and technicians and they became great tankers.

The tanks in 1940, manned by converted infantry and cavalrymen, were still being called "combat cars". They were armed only with machine guns, most of them with a gun in each of two turrets. Weighing only eight or nine tons, they could easily make 65 mph, their governors tampered with by the mechanics while the offi-

cers looked the other way. This speed and the noise did relieve to some extent the impotence of some of the newer tanks which had big holes in the fronts of the turrets, waiting for the installation of 37 mm cannon. The older tanks were rapidly becoming obsolete but had contributed much experience to several units descended from famous old World War I outfits which had been incorporated into the new 2nd Armored Division. There were even some World War I veterans present, including George S. Patton himself, the brigade commander and soon to become division commander.

T1E1 demonstrating its obstacle crossing abilities. Only 1 T1E1 was produced, built by the Ordnance Department in 1925. (Oregon Historical Military Museum)

Left:
Christie T3 Combat Car. The T3 was introduced in 1931 by J. Walter Christie, with total production reaching seven vehicles. Christie failed to win an American contract for full scale production, though he did succeed in selling his design to Great Britain and the Soviet Union. The British based their Cruiser tanks on this design while the Soviets developed the BT series tank.

Right:
T3E2 (American La France Tank) on display at Ft. Benning, September 1940. This vehicle also was designed by J. Walter Christie and was produced in 1933.

Left:
M1 Combat Car. This vehicle was developed in 1935 and was the forerunner of the M2, M3 and M5 light tanks series.

Left:
Nice close up view of an M2A3. Future vehicles would be based on this vehicle's hull and chassis. Ft. Owens, 1939.
(Hylinski Collection)

Below:
M2A2 and M2A3 tanks on ex-cercise. This photo clearly shows two variants of the M2. The vehicle in the foreground, an M2A2, has round-ed turrets while the vehicle on the left of the photo, an M2A3, has square edged tur-rets. Ft. Owens, 1939.
(Hylinski Collection)

Above: Over the top! An in action view of an M2A2 negotiating a hill at speed. Ft. Owens, 1937. (Hylinski Collection)

Below: An impressive collection of M2A2 and M2A3 tanks in formation. Ft. Owens, 1937. (Hylinski Collection)

Left:
M2A3 traveling at speed during maneuvers at Ft. Benning, 1941.
(Stalker Collection)

Below:
Old and the new. This picture illustrates the commonality of hulls between the twin-turreted M2A3 and M2A4 light tanks.
(Stalker Collection)

This prophetic photo illustrates 2nd Cavalry troops being overtaken by a motorized column.

What is an Echelon?

Many of us knew nothing of the organization of an armored division. The lower ranks cared little about such boring details. But those of us assigned, by accident or design, to the 2nd Armored BRIGADE soon knew that we were the main STRIKING echelon of the division and found that it contained the brigade headquarters, a headquarters company, a whole regiment of artillery and the **guts of the division--three tank regiments**--the 66th and 68th (light tanks) and the 67th (medium tanks).

We were proud in our brigade but were aware that orders did come from somewhere higher up, the COMMAND echelon. This contained division headquarters, a headquarters company and a signal company, the nerve center of the division.

Everybody knows that you have to study the terrain and find the enemy, to look before you leap. For that purpose, our RECONNAISSANCE echelon was big, strong and fast, an entire battalion plus an attached airplane observation squadron.

The SUPPORT echelon was everything else that could be involved in the front ranks of battle: an entire rifle regiment, a field artillery battalion, an engineer battalion and an attached tank destroyer battalion.

Soon we also recognized the contributions of the SERVICE echelon: an ordnance battalion (weapons), a quartermaster battalion (supply) and a medical battalion (for the sick and wounded). This completed a roster of 15,000 men, **a complete miniature army built around a tank brigade.**

All echelons were entirely motorized, riding in nearly 3000 large vehicles and 810 motorcycles (before we had jeeps) and requiring 80 miles of road space on a non-tactical march, taking 3 to 4 hours to pass a given point. The 1st Armored Division was the same size but the 14 later armored divisions had only 12,000 men.

Left:
Lt. Malcolm J. Stalker (in foreground) leads a group of motorcycles along a tank trail, Ft. Benning, March 1941. Stalker was the Liaison Officer between the 66th Armored Regiment and division headquarters. He received a commendation from General Patton for establishing standards of excellence in his inspired collection and dissemination of information, one of many examples of the long lasting benefits of individual dedication in the 2nd Armored Division.
(Stalker Collection)

Below:
Before the jeeps. Messenger and liaison motorcycles at 2nd Armored Division H.Q., 1941.
(Stalker Collection)

M3A1 White Scout Cars on the move during training at Ft. Benning, Sept., 1940. Notice the use of service caps, goggles, and dust masks by the crew. Pioneer tools are carried in brackets. With the governor disconnected, a scout car could be pushed to 70 mph on a road.

Machine Gun Company

An initial assignment as a platoon leader in machine guns in the 66th Armored Regiment was more glamorous and challenging than I expected it to be. The Machine Gun Company of each tank regiment had great mobility and more fire power than an entire old style infantry regiment!

The missions of the Machine Gun Company were aggressive and daring, including advance guard, often putting us out in front, to find and engage the enemy; small arms support with or between tank formations; and security, for resting units or as flank protection on the move.

We rapidly learned the uses of speed.

There were three platoons of five scout cars each, plus headquarters vehicles, all scout cars bristling with .30 and .50 caliber machine guns, plus other individual weapons, 14 weapons in all per car. These 4-wheel drive cars had 1/4 inch armor and bullet-proof self-sealing tires with very heavy mastic-filled inner tubes which could be changed only with special equipment. The fronts of these open cars, as in the half-tracks soon to replace them, had armored radiator louvers, cantilevered rollers for crossing ditches or winches with long steel cables.

Machine gun company scout car crew wearing jodhpur pants and field caps. Ft. Benning, Sept., 1940.

Uniforms

In 1940, armor officers were still wearing the old cavalry jodhpur pants and boots, but these were soon eliminated as being silly in armored vehicles. Some of us suspected the old cavalry officers would have liked to put saddles on the tank turrets. In the field, armor officers proudly wore leather jackets espoused by General Patton until higher authorities banned them. The traditional rubber-haloed crash helmets were replaced later by head gear resembling a football helmet, standard from then on. These helmets had ventilating holes in them, and had attachments for radio headphones, microphones, goggles, ventilating flaps and neck and jaw protectors. The standard steel helmet, without its liner, would fit over the crash helmet for protection in the turret hatch or when out of the tank.

Our garrison uniform was like any other soldier's but, in the field, armor troops wore coveralls with many pockets, overseas caps (if not the helmets) and the standard G.I. shoes. Canvas leggings were worn at times and ammunition belts added for carrying extra items. A platoon leader could be loaded with field glasses, compass, canteen, a holstered .45 automatic pistol, first aid packet, whistle and message book. Some of this stuff was stored in his vehicle when riding.

Capt. Richard Hunt wearing a characteristic U.S. Cavalry uniform. The U.S. Army soon discovered how impractical the jodhpur pants were in tanks and discontinued their use for tank crews. Many officers did continue to wear them for dress. Ft. Benning, Sept., 1940.

Lt. Worthen Dustin Muzzey wearing overalls and World War I style steel helmet. Ft. Benning, Jan., 1941.

Lt. Muzzey's pipe and posture in the photo above have nothing to do with uniforms but his style does evoke memories of what we learned about the kind of blood flowing in his veins, the kind we liked in the 2nd Armored Division. When his ancestress, Hannah Dustin, with her newborn child and a nurse, was kidnapped by Indians in Massachusetts in 1697, she, with the aid of the nurse and a captive English boy, tomahawked and scalped 10 Indians and escaped. (Encylopaedia Brittanica)

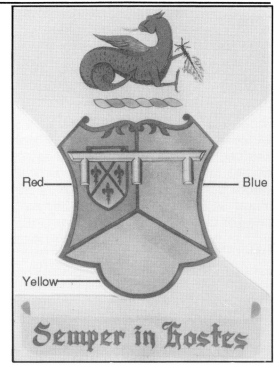

Above:
Coat of Arms - 66th Armored Regiment.

Right:
66 A.R. brass lapel insignia - actual size.

Left:
Lt. Perkins wearing a leather jacket espoused by Gen. George S. Patton. The jackets were later discontinued by the War Department. Notice the patch of the 66th Armored Regiment on the left side of the jacket. Ft. Benning, Jan., 1941.

Short History of Tanks of The Second Armored Division

The tank history was closely associated with that of all descendants of the American Tank Corps in World War I. In the 66th Armored Regiment, the 2nd Battalion's ancestors were the 301st and 344th Tank Battalions, and the 3rd Battalion's, the 328th Battalion. These, with an ancestor of the 1st Battalion of the 68th Armored Regiment became the 1st Tank Regiment. In 1932 it was renamed 66th Infantry (Light Tanks). On July 15, 1940 the 66th was designated 66th Armored Regiment (Light) and on August 1, 1940 other necessary new units were activated. The 67th had similar ancestry. Later changes affecting the three tank regiments are described on page 85.

Insignia of the 66th Armored Regiment - 1940

The Coat of Arms of the 66th symbolizes the complex family tree. The red, yellow, and blue represent the Artillery, Cavalry and Infantry, the original sources of the American Tank Corps. The small shield in the upper right of the main shield is the Coat of Arms of the city of Langres, France where part of this unit was organized. The label, a bar with three point suspension, indicates that the 66th was heir-apparent, inheriting the proud traditions of the Tankers of the A.E.F. Above the shield crouches the fabulous medieval monster, the Wyvern, whose glance is death. The Wyvern, symbol of the tank, goes through fire, crushes, destroys. Its head turns to the right, in heraldry meaning victory. The motto, "Semper in Hostes" means "Always into the enemy."

Pulling the final drive of an M2A4 during a 3 month tank maintenance course for officers at Ft. Knox, March, 1941.

The Armored Force School

During the early days of the 2nd Armored Division thousands of men were given a great variety of formal courses of instruction, ranging from cooks, bakers and barbers, to the whole gamut of technical skills such as automotive and radio repairs and maintenance. At the same time, hundreds of officers were groomed for special roles. Their schools, too, were broad in scope but tended more to management, not only in preparation for command and staff functions later, but to qualify for close involvement in technical matters. I chose a 3-month tank maintenance course at Fort Knox, Kentucky, beginning in February, 1941, because I wanted to get into the tanks.

The Armored Force School wisely combined

our mechanical training with a general review of all the basic combat principles as applied to armor, anticipating that we would not remain in fixed assignments. This intensive schooling was a balance of classroom and shop work. We had to pass exams on such subjects as the basic missions of armor, the logistics of supply and transportation, march and bivouac security, combat orders, the echelons of attack, communication and control and the uses of space, time and speed.

It was possible to get sleepy in some of these classes. In fact, I took a photo of two men sleeping and snoring through a motorcycle maintenance class. But it was not hard to remember such precepts as "Once you gain contact

Pulling the 7 cylinder, air cooled, Continental radial engine.

with the enemy, never lose that contact; advance against resistance, pursue and destroy".

New practical experiences were diverse, including training in night vision, radio voice discipline, and the principles of camouflage. We were exposed to the use of special training devices and aptitude tests for gunnery and other specialties, and when it came to delving into the guts of a tank we were very much awake. **What a complex realm is a tank!**

The tank maintenance shops did not make mechanics out of the officers but we did develop a close familiarity with engines, power trains, suspension systems, tracks, turrets, tank guns, gyro-stabilizers, lubrication, cooling and the electrical systems.

The disciplines and routines of trouble shooting were an intellectual challenge. The instructor would sabotage one or more of the four major electrical systems in a tank and we were required to find and correct the defects rapidly, as in battle. We even had to draw a diagram of a voltage regulator and pass tests on valve and ignition timing and know all the causes of high temperature or low oil pressure. After these three months we were speaking a new language.

The excitement of applying all this knowledge by now was only a few weeks ahead of us. Our adventures were soon to begin.

Above: Preparing the engine for installation.

Below: Troubleshooting the electrical systems.

Above: Hooking up the engine.

Below: Part of the training included the dismantling and reassembly of the M2A4's suspension.

Above: Back together and running.

Below: Washing off the dirt and mud after a successful road test.

Co. H M2A4 light tanks, lined up for Saturday inspection. Ft. Benning May, 1941.

Tank Company

On return to Ft. Benning, I happily transferred to Co. H, 3rd Battalion, 66th Armored Regiment (light tanks.) Each of the three tank regiments in the division had three battalions of three tank companies each. The 66th and other units proudly carried the colors in their crests from battle streamers of World War I.

I soon discovered my good luck. This very prestigious company was descended from a World War I tank unit that had been on continuous active duty ever since. First Sergeant Nethken was only the third First Sergeant in the company since World War I when the original ancestor of Co. H was Co. C, 1st Separate Battalion, Heavy Tank Service, 65th Engineers, created in Feb., 1918 at Camp Upton, New York. Its further evolution occurred in the battalions described on page 23.

There were old group photographs on the barracks walls of tanks and men of the 1930s. Corporal Harold W. Roberts of a sister company evolved from Co. C in World War I had won the Congressional Medal of Honor in France where his tank rolled over into a shell hole full of water and he shoved his crew out before he drowned. Camp Roberts in California was named for him. Another Medal of Honor winner in the same battalion was Corporal Donald M. Call. It was even more remarkable that 23 Distinguished Service Crosses were won by these first American tankers! There were hints that the ardor of the older non-coms was being passed on to the new recruits and perhaps it would not have surprised many if they could have known in advance that there would be another Medal of Honor winner, Captain James Burt, who took command of Company H in the European campaign of World War II.

Above: Lt. Perkins (left) and Lt. McConnell wearing typical clothing and gear for tankers in 1940. Lt. Perkins is wearing the early rubber haloed tanker's helmet and dual filtered dust mask. Notice the 2nd Armored patch is worn in different places (Lt. Perkins, on his pocket and Lt. McConnell, above his pocket), which suggests this had not been standardized yet. Ft. Benning, April, 1941.

Below: A 'D' Company M2A4. (Stalker Collection)

Cranking up at dawn for a day in the field. Ft. Benning, April, 1941.

The Mystique Of Tanks

For a neophyte like me, entering a tank park for the first time was a thrill. With the dawn mist just clearing, you walked over to a tank and felt the chill of cold armor against your palm. Then, as the air-cooled radial engines cranked up, blue smoke filled the park, the ground shook, and you didn't care that all that pollution could be shortening your life, because this was life! The tanks would leave the tank park with a churning roar of gunned motors, while increasing speed smoothed out the heavy clanking of sprockets. The typical classical squeaking of the tracks could often be heard farther away than the motors. This squeaking has been the signature sound of American tanks for many years.

At the end of a day in the field, there was a distinct camaraderie among the dismounting tank crews in their dirty jumpsuits, faces streaked with dust and sweat, dragging out their personal equipment, stretching their limbs and unconsciously swaggering with the feeling of accomplishment. As a young officer I respected the veteran enlisted tankers; they knew the ropes and were my teachers.

Riding In A Tank

In the four-man light tank crew, the driver and the bow gunner-assistant driver had the best seats because it was like sitting in a rocking chair, close to the bottom of the tank. Up in the turret, the tank commander and gunner had it a lot rougher because, with the rolling or pitching of the tank on rough ground, they could get slammed around, in danger of concussion or broken ribs. They could either sit or stand in the turret. The commander usually could look out and brace himself for what was coming, but the gunner had to keep braced all of the time, afraid to risk his face against the vision ports. On maneuvers and road marches, padded goggles and dust masks were used, even by the driver and bow gunner, because they often drove with their hatches open for better vision, unless in simulated combat. All wore safety belts.

Above: Factory fresh M2A4. This vehicle displayed America's awakening to modern tank design. Though still bristling with machine guns which suggested infantry support, the design actually implied the use of independent tank group tactics.

Right: This gold washed sterling silver pin was purchased at the Ft. Benning PX by Lt. Perkins as the first and most appropriate jewelry for his future wife (enlarged 3.3x).

The M2A4 Light Tank

This 11-1/2 ton (later heavier) tank, developed in 1940, delivered to us in 1941, was powerful, fast and nimble, like a leopard. Any man who developed a knack for the inertia and rhythms of heavy vehicles found this tank a real joy to drive. But he had to learn that cowboy-type handling could throw a track. It replaced the obsolete M2A1, M2A2 and M2A3, none of which was used in combat. It cost $30,000 to $35,000, the 7 cylinder radial air cooled Continental engine alone, $8,000. Its road radius was 130 miles.

The M2A4 had a slightly thicker armor but still only 25 mm in front. It had a single fully rotating turret, mounting a 37 mm cannon, instead of the previous twin turrets, and five air-cooled machine guns. Three of these were hull mounted, a fixed one pointing forward from each side sponson, fired by the driver, aiming the whole tank (like a fighter plane pilot) and one ball-mounted in the right anterior slope plate, fired by the bow gunner, watching his tracers through his vision slot. The cannon and a coaxially mounted machine gun in the cannon mantlet were fired by the gunner, using a tubular gun sight in the mantlet. The tank commander had to load these guns and he also operated an outside turret-mounted anti-aircraft machine gun. A hand crank traversed the turret and its guns but the gunner, wrapped around the shoulder guard, moved and aimed them like he would a rifle or shotgun. There were separate triggers for the cannon and machine gun.

Above: Using camouflage techniques to hide an M2A4 in the pine forests of Ft. Benning. April, 1941.

Below: Washing up the M2A4s. This was part of preventive maintenance. Notice that the main gun is missing on H-10. This was due to a shortage in production of 37 mm guns.

Preparing for the Tennessee Maneuvers. Ft. Benning, May, 1941.

When the Division was activated on 15 July 1940, it was constituted as follows
and with the following officers commanding its major forces.

Second Armored Division
Commanded by Major General Charles L Scott
Division Headquarters and Headquarters Company
Division Service Company
48th Signal Company

Second Armored Brigade
Commanded by Brigadier General George S. Patton, Jr.
66th Armored Regiment (Light)
67th Armored Regiment (Medium)
68th Armored Regiment (Light)

Division Control
41st Armored Infantry Regiment
14th Field Artillery Regiment (Armored)
78th Field Artillery Battalion (Armored)
2d Reconnaissance Battalion
17th Engineer Battalion (Armored)
17th Ordnance Battalion
14th Quartermaster Battalion (Armored)
48th Medical Battalion

The effect of prolonged tank rides is evident on the faces of these two crewmen. (Young Collection)

Accident Prevention, A Tanker's Commandments

Tank in motion. Keep hips below top of turret; always a man in the turret on roads; door securely open or shut; hands off turret opening; guns and turret locked in position (non-combat); no loose tools; keep sponson clear for ventilation; safety belts; helmets always worn; never back-track in woods or on soft ground; close front doors on towed tank; no unnecessary riding outside; foot troops stand when tanks moving nearby.

Guiding. One guide only whether single tank or group of tanks; guide where he can see everything; not too close (especially at night); don't get between tank and wall, post or another vehicle; don't fall down.

General. Enter and exit from front (unless guns are armed); no smoking in or on tank; never lie or sleep near tank; never run motor over one minute indoors; do all mechanical checking before starting and as otherwise prescribed; fire extinguishers in hand for refueling; avoid fuel on skin; cleanliness; no sloppy or unsecured stowage.

An M2A4 kicking up the dust during a cross country run at Ft. Benning, Sept., 1941.

Control

Before we received FM radios and intercoms in November 1941, platoon leaders controlled their other tanks with flag and hand signals. The tank commander, either a sergeant or an officer, controlled his driver with foot signals, pressing between his shoulder blades to move out or speed up, on the top of his head to slow down or stop, and on one shoulder to turn right or left. Tapping was commonly used for backing up.

Driver's Panic. During one night tank maneuver in the pine woods at Ft. Benning, my young driver panicked, froze on the throttle and would respond only to foot signals to turn right or left . In the dark of the moon and heavy dust, I could scarcely see the trees and tried to steer him away from them. We were zig zagging all over the woods at top speed, crisscrossing a dirt road. Finally I lost control of him and we ran into a 10-inch pine tree. I instantly ducked, according to standard practice, the tree was knocked down, and about 15 feet of the dead top broke off and landed squarely across the turret hatch where my head had been. We had a vigorous verbal exchange after that about his bone head and my heavy foot.

In May, 1941 in a shake down maneuver in the northern part of Ft. Benning reservation, under simulated combat conditions, four men were killed in the first four days and there were 21 bones broken in five days. Most of the casualties were motorcyclists. We did perhaps $2,000 worth of damage to vehicles in our company alone, but with field repairs we kept them all going.

All crew members had vision slots but there were extra vision ports in the turret and cupola. It was not pleasant to think of getting a face full of bullets through the slots. The air-cooled seven-cylinder radial Continental engine in the rear would drive this tank at 30-40 mph on good ground and, with the governor disconnected, could reach at least 65 mph on a road. The tank commander in the left side of the turret could easily reach the driver with his foot for signaling but, until we got intercoms, loud voice commands had to be used if the turret was turned very far. The whole tank would be turned if more convenient than hand traversing the turret.

Repairing the clutch in an M2A4. The motor (right of picture) was pulled using the derrick at the rear of the truck. Ft. Benning, April, 1941.

Field Maintenance And Field Expedients

The tank crews themselves had many skills but the company maintenance section added the expertise of real mechanics. We could pull the radial engine out of a light tank in 35 minutes and replace it in 90 minutes, in the field, using a maintenance truck with a derrick.

Probably the most common field problem was restoring a thrown track. The large sprockets in front pulled the track forward over rollers and a large idler wheel in the rear. The track was kept pretty taut and didn't slip off the rollers or idler. A track most often was thrown by a tank turning too quickly in soft ground or sand which would push the track down away from the bogey wheels and slip it off to one side. Sometimes, if the maintenance crew was not nearby, we could restore the track to its proper position by digging a trench under each side of the tank, one trench under the thrown track to give room to work on it, and the other trench to cause the tank to tip to the opposite side, belly-ing it on the ground. This sometimes made it possible to maneuver the thrown track back under the bogey wheels. Sometimes power could be applied to the sprockets to run the track back on. Then another tank could drag the stuck tank out of the dug trenches onto hard ground.

More commonly, though, we used our tools to "break" the track, in preparation for the maintenance crew to restore it with heavier equipment, sometimes towing the tank off of and then back onto the track before reconnecting it. Each track weighed 1600 pounds, so it was hard for several men to manhandle it. Without the maintenance crew, the tank could be towed back onto the straightened track by another tank, then, using the tow cable wrapped around the sprocket as a winch, the rest of the track could be pulled up over the idler and top rollers to the front to be reattached.

On one occasion, a tank broke through a crust over mushy ground at Ft. Benning, so markedly tipping the tank that it had to be dragged out by three other tanks in tandem, using their inch-thick tow cables. This gouged a huge V-shaped trench over a hundred yards long which I suspect is still a terrain feature there. It was a worse problem in the swamps of Louisiana in the 1941 maneuvers.

"Blown bogies" were a common occurrence. Part or all of the hard rubber tire would separate from the steel wheel, usually causing a noise or bumping. Within 10-30 minutes, using jacks and wrenches, we could replace the wheel. Spare bogies were carried on the outside of the hull. There was more of this kind of trouble when tanks were made heavier with appliquéd armor or with improvised other kinds of added protection. Normally a rubber shoed track would last 1200 miles on each side of the reversible shoes.

A camouflaged M2A4. Notice how the branches have been placed in order to conceal this vehicle. Ft. Benning. April, 1941.

Using obsolete tanks for tank obstacle testing. The M2A3 has leaped over the tank obstacle. Ft. Knox, April, 1941.

Tank Obstacles

At the Armored Force School, Ft. Knox, in early 1941, we found that even light tanks could breach different kinds of above-ground obstacles if built only of braced heavy logs and pilings. Some would be driven into the ground or shattered if hit at high speed, and the tank could actually leap over them, sometimes jumping 20 or 30 feet. Medium tanks simply smashed them to pieces and tended to bounce off and over the better-constructed obstacles. On the other hand, a deep, broad pit wider than the spanning ability of the tank tracks would stop them.

This time the M2A3 has been caught at the moment of impact. Notice the slack in the track from the shock of hitting the obstacle. Ft. Knox, April, 1941.

M2 halftrack and 75 mm gun of the 78th Field Artillery on the move . The crew are still wearing the World War I style steel helmet. Notice the water cooled .30 cal. machine gun and communication wire spools. The usual pioneer tools are carried.

Halftracks

These replaced most of the armored 4-wheeled scout cars. We had three of them in each tank company, one for the company commander as a command vehicle and two for the maintenance section. Although weighing 8-3/4 tons, they could go 45 mph on a road or up to 55 mph with the governor disconnected and could follow a tank anywhere cross country. The 1/4 inch armor could stop a .30 caliber bullet but not .50 caliber at right angles. Front wheel power was used when needed for added traction.

The command halftrack was fitted for map reading, reconnaissance functions and for control. Radios were added later. There was a powerful heater for cold weather and a canvas top in case of heavy rain.

The crew consisted of a driver, a .50 caliber machine gunner, two .30 caliber machine gunners, a rifleman, a radio operator and a car commander, in addition to any officer who might choose to ride in it. Although the company maintenance officer might stay either with one of his halftracks or in the tank retriever in combat, the company commander customarily took to his command tank for combat.

Gen. George S. Patton (right) narrates a maneuver held for Secretary of War Henry L. Stimson (standing). Several miniature Blitzkriegs were held for foreign generals and dignitaries. Ft. Benning, Dec., 1940.

Patton's Tactical Principles

Patton had a remarkable talent for expressing combat principles in simple language. His incessant harping on them was legendary. The basic ones: "Grab 'em by the nose and kick 'em in the ass" (fire and maneuver). "If you get lost behind the enemy lines and are confused, go burn a village." "Don't have any compassion for the enemy. The first time you're in battle you're going to feel bad about killing somebody but remember these guys are the Huns who raped your mother and sister." "If you are confused and scared in the attack, all you've got to remember is that the enemy is more scared than you are if you are attacking." About the speed of the attack, he said, "When you have a carefully planned attack, with all of the flank guards, advance guard and support arranged, and the reserve all planned, don't worry about

the details - attack with the utmost speed and audacity. You will have more casualties per hour but fewer casualties per day." "You young lieutenants have got to realize that your platoon is like a piece of spaghetti; you can't push it, you've got to get out in front and pull it." "I expect every one of you lieutenants to return a conqueror or a corpse."

At one of his indoctrination meetings for the 600 officers of the division, Patton read us a very long soliloquy he had written about the bayonet, taking it from the forge into the guts of the enemy. He stated that "You young officers have got to get used to the idea that there are going to be blood and guts all over the battlefield". He spontaneously was named "Old Blood and Guts".

A Tanker's Fraternity

Anti-Machine Gun League

Order of the Little Red Tank

ANTI-MACHINE GUN LEAGUE

Order of the Little Red Tank

Tank Chapter No. 1

HISTORY

It is appropriate upon the initiation of each new member to the Order of the Little Red Tank that he fully understand the significance and history of the order.

The Order of the Little Red Tank and Chapter Number One of the Anti-Machine Gun League was organized at Ft. Benning, Georgia in December, 1933 by LT. COL. JOHN H. STUTESMAN Commanding Officer 2d Battalion 66th Infantry (Light Tanks) from October 2, 1933 to October 1, 1935, at a private party at his quarters just before Christmas 1933 at which were present those officers of 2d Battalion 66th Infantry (Light Tanks) on duty at that time with the Battalion.

The order was activated with the view of organizing a society which only "Tankers" and their higher commanders in the chain of command would be eligible*. The insignia of the order was a small toy, red colored, tank (Originally of the Model 1917 Renault tank used by the first American tank units during World War One of 1914 - 1918). The motto selected for the order was the Latin phrase - "Surom Conda", the literal translation of which is "Let your tails be lifted up", and idiomatically translated by the first Grand Master as "Keep your tails up"! The color red of the insignia is heraldic of the bravery of those tankers gone before, and symbolic of the terror which tanks, on the field of battle, strike into the hearts of the foes of our country, and principles for which our country stands.

C, H, BRAGG
Lt. Col., 66th Armored Regiment
Grand Master.

/alc

(To be given to each new member on initiation into the order)

* Officers were appointed Knights and enlisted men Squires at appropriate times both before and after going overseas.

Chapter 2

Tennessee Maneuvers - June, 1941

This was the acid test of the great power and mobility of the 2nd Armored Division. Some 78,000 men were involved for two weeks, the largest combined arms maneuver that had ever been held in the United States. The 2nd Armored Division made at least four long road marches of a hundred miles or more under cover of darkness, to attack at dawn from a predetermined assembly position. In each case, we were up all day, all night and all the next day. The tanks and other track-laying vehicles travelled from Ft. Benning to northern Tennessee by rail, while the wheeled vehicle "trains" went by road. One tank march was 140 miles, most of it under cover of darkness, the first 70-80 miles by good but dangerous highways through mountains. One tank missed a curve, hit a cliff and killed all four men in the crew.

Our new diesel light tanks could travel 200-240 miles on about 79 gallons per full tank. Ordinarily the tanks would be sent by rail if over 50 miles in peace time, or 200 miles in war time. The wheels usually went by road. If all went by train, an armored division required about 120 trains.

After loading M2A4 light tanks on railroad flatcars, chock blocks are placed as part of the preparation for transport to Tennessee.

Left:
An M3 Stuart taking its turn loading on a railroad flatcar train. The riveted turret indicates that this is from the original first production batch of M3 light tanks. The large rear idler wheel is quite noticeable in this photo, giving more ground contact. Because the flatcars were already hooked together, all tanks would go up the same ramp and drive forward from car to car, the first ones going the length of the train, easily spanning the spaces between cars. Notice the pioneer tools on the tank.

Below:
Loaded and on their way to Tennessee.

H-3, victim of a crash into the Caney River Bridge, which tore off the front sprocket and housing. The tank was returned to the factory for repairs. The crew survived with minor injuries.

Accidents

Our memories linger on some spectacular accidents. The 3rd Battalion of the 66th had its share. It was last in column in a fast night march in Tennessee, using little blue blackout headlights which lit the road for only a few yards ahead, invisible to an airplane. As one H Company tank drove onto a high bridge over the Caney River, the driver, blinded by an approaching civilian automobile's headlights, "touched" his right steering lever to give the civilian more room and hit the concrete railing at about 45 mph. The right front sprocket tore down 20 or 30 feet of concrete in a great shower of sparks. This tore out the sprocket, broke the track, wrenched out the final drive shaft and housing, sprung the suspension system and even warped the hull of the tank as it leaped into the air, fell on its left side,

swung around and completely blocked the bridge roadway, gently rocking for a few moments.

Temporarily in command of the battalion trains, I came upon the scene in my jeep moments later. My dim blue blackout lights, added to the blue lights of other tanks, revealed a shocking sight, with the upturned bulk of the tank, great chunks of concrete and debris strewn upon the roadbed, and soon a silently investigating ambulance crew, aided by helmeted tankers. Everything was the same weird, blue-gray color. Only the tank commander was slightly injured and they were all laughing.

We used another tank to drag the wreckage out of the way, clearing one lane. A few min-

One of the more spectacular accidents in the Tennessee Maneuvers. This tank from Co. I literally brought down City Hall.

utes later another tank driver, squeezing by, accidently locked one steering lever in the middle of the bridge, crashed through the railing and teetered frightfully on the edge, 100 feet above the river. With presence of mind, he locked his other lever too, and the crew crawled out while we hitched another tank to it and dragged it back to safety.

Another sequel to the bridge accident was The Wild Ride of Captain Lumpkin. As H Company Commander, he was trying to catch the tail of the regiment miles ahead of him. With the engine governor "fixed", he was traveling about 60 mph and only one other tank had stuck with him. I found one tank crew by the side of the road who said they had been unable to keep up and had simply given up. At 65 mph in my jeep I finally caught him several miles farther along. The blue lights of my jeep and of the one

following tank revealed a beautiful phosphorescent monstrosity. The roaring 1,600 pound tracks, whipping forward to the sprockets at twice the speed of the tank, were undulating wickedly along the tops of the idler rollers, like giant glowing eels out of the *Ancient Mariner*, laced with static electricity. Red and blue fire from the twin exhausts and the unmuffled roar of the motor completed the picture. At considerable risk, I got past him and slowed him down with flashlight signals.

A wonderful accident occurred in Bell Buckle, a county seat in Tennessee, where we were going through a long S-curve in the center of town. A delivery truck got in the way and a tank driver avoided it by driving up on a sidewalk. This rocked the tank, he lost control, and the tank slid along the front of the two-story

Destroying a barnyard!

brick wall of the City Hall. The left brush guard took out two or three courses of brick along the wall, whereupon all two stories of it collapsed and fell into the street and onto the tank. The second story floor, lacking its support, sagged, and the furniture slid out and fell onto the street around the tank. The only person hurt was the tank commander, with a little bruise on his head. We uncovered the tank and it drove away. The locals were impressed.

One I Company tank driver on a blackout march thought a row of mailboxes and a tree were on the left side of the road. Actually, they were on the right and when he went to the right of them in the dark, he broke through a fence, entered a farmyard full of equipment and destroyed plows, rakes, seeders and a bailer and proceeded back out through the fence onto the

road, radioing that they had "hit a fence or something". I stopped and dragged a wagon axle and a wheel out of the road before proceeding. Radio conversations between tanks on this march included some very weird, plaintive and gloriously foolish remarks. These were CW radios which could be used for short range voice transmission.

Later in this maneuver, while crashing through a pine forest with our tanks, it was fascinating to watch the once-cocky foot troops frantically scattering as the giant whips of falling trees beat the woods and underbrush ahead of us and flushed them out. Grievances caused by infractions of rules and disputed umpire decisions brought about fist fights, fixing of bayonets and firing of tinfoil pellets from blank cartridges. A fine time was had by all.

One day the 66th rolled over eight tanks into ditches, teaching us a proper respect for soft shoulders on country roads. One night tank H-8, 66th Armored, fell about eight feet off of a wooden bridge when its lights shorted out. It lodged against the bridge pillars and three 18-ton wrecker trucks were required to pull it out and tip it up. While waiting for them, one country Jake came up and offered his Model A Ford to help pull them out, while another man started after his team of mules! After the Tennessee maneuvers, as Battalion Investigating Officer, I had to collect 109 reports, statements and findings to make recommendations for only three accidents that occurred in our battalion involving damaged property. All citizens and local governments were paid for damage to private and public property.

The people of Tennessee seemed to be thrilled, cooperative and proud of our army. Motorists threw candy and food to the men. Many of the women were quite emotional and exchanged notes and addresses with us.

A series of four old men added a charming social ambience to our rural invasions. One of them, watching a tank battalion fording a river said, "I didn't know we had that many tanks! Why don't we attack Hitler now?" Another, standing in a village square, waiting for his daughter who worked in a soda fountain near a carnival, was afraid to go there "because Hitler drops bombs on people in crowds." At a rest halt along a country road, a feeble old man doggedly carried out buckets of water to us. It was bad tasting "sulfur water" but we din't have the heart to refuse it.

In a fourth incident a tank crashed through a fence and corn field and stopped next to a farm house. The hot grimy-faced tank commander pulled off his goggles and found he could have jumped onto the porch beside a surprised old gentleman who blinked his eyes, went inside and came out with a bucket of water.

These incidents occurred in or near towns with names like Hoodoo, Fudge Around, Daylight, Gnat Hill, Sheybogan, and Grace's Folly.

Short break in the maneuvers. Lt. Perkins is wearing full tanker's field gear, including a double filtered dust mask and a gas mask under his left arm.

Left:
This unfortunate M3 discovered the perils of soft shouldered roads. Eight tanks of the 66th Regiment rolled over on this day.

Right:
It took two light tanks to pull 3-2 out again.

The original "jeep", 1941 Dodge T202-VC1 command car.

Jeeps

Our first extensive use of jeeps was made in the Tennessee maneuvers. The original "Jeeps" were the big 4-wheeled command and reconnaissance (C&R) cars, nicknamed for a comic strip character in "Popeye The Sailor Man". When these were phased out, the new little quarter-ton trucks which had at first been called "peeps" or "blitz buggies" soon became jeeps. These were remarkably versatile. Power on all four wheels could take them almost anywhere a tank could go except through a wall, and some places a tank could not go. The top speed was 75 mph.

The jeep had synchromesh 3 speeds ahead and a reverse. An extra shift lever on the floor doubled all these choices with a compound low range. There was no differential between the front and rear axles, so for hard surface roads another lever changed the 4-wheel to 2-wheel drive, reducing the strain on the power trains and tires on curves or sharper turning.

Far superior to a motorcycle in almost everything, they could traverse rough ground, go up and down stairways and climb very steep hills. They were used for communication, reconnaissance, convoy control, advance party work, approach marches and as prime movers for small cannon. We often carried equipment, supplies or meals in them. When equipped with machine guns on pedestals, they became moving machine gun nests. Convertible tops and side curtains could be used in bad weather.

Six hours after the bridge wreck, we were in a jeep following a tank on a very dusty road. We had to stop suddenly and the tired driver of the following tank ran over the left rear corner of the jeep, smashed the body, destroyed the rear wheel and tire and threw the car off the road against a stump. Two of us managed to jump out in time, but the driver had his back bruised when his seat was jammed against the steering wheel. After replacing the destroyed wheel with our spare and straightening out our seats a little, we went on our way, marvelling at the toughness of these little 2,600 pound cars.

The successor to the Dodge jeep, the 1941 Willys MA "peep", later called "jeep".

In 1940 the U.S. Army realized that the Dodge command car was too heavy and visualized the need for a light command/reconnaissance vehicle with good mobility on varying terrains. The U.S. Ordnance Technical Committee released requirements for such a vehicle weighing 1300 lbs or less with four wheel drive and a load capacity of 600 lbs. A deadline of 75 days was set and several automobile and engineering companies were contacted. The American Bantam Car Company and Willys-Overland Motors responded but only Bantam managed to complete their model by the deadline and received the initial contract. It was soon discovered the Bantam vehicle was underpowered and fragile so Willys was given an opportunity. Working in conjunction with the U.S. Army Quartermaster Corps, and not being concerned with the military specification for weight requirements, Willys produced a more robust and powerful vehicle. This vehicle was tested in Nov. 1940 and was considered a complete success, though still too heavy by government standards.

The U.S. was anxious to get a vehicle of this type into production, so they raised the weight restrictions to 2641 lbs. Bantam, Willys, and now Ford, presented new models for testing. The Bantam and Ford versions met the requirements but were grossly underpowered. The Willys variant had almost twice the power of the Bantam and Ford vehicles but still did not meet the weight requirements. The U.S. government would not budge on the weight specifications so Willys trimmed their design until their vehicle met with the government's approval. Therefore, they were awarded the contract and started production of 16,000 vehicles in early 1941. The eventual load capacity was 600 lbs. cross country and 1200 lbs. on roads.

The initial vehicles were designated MA and when larger fuel tanks were installed to meet a requirement for longer ranging, the designation was changed to MB. Ford was contracted to manufacture the Willys Model MB which was designated 1/4 Ton, 4 x 4 Ford Model GPW.

After two days and two nights of constant movement, the troops get to rest. Cowan, Tennessee

Life In The Field

During the most strenuous phase of the maneuvers, we learned to sleep on anything from a turret to a bramble, eat rough meals prepared in the dark, and shave at night with leftover hot coffee instead of water. We studied maps and charted routes by flashlight and coordinated eating, maintenance, refueling, setting up local security and bivouacs. When issuing orders, we tried to allow the men as much sleep as possible. Going without sleep was part of the hardening process.

A tank company commander issues orders to his men. (U.S. Army)

Above:
Notice the effect on the suspension of this M2A4 while it negotiates its descent. Also notice the pioneering equipment stowage.

Left:
Harley Davidson motorcycle and M2A4. Note the arrangement of jerry cans on the rear of the tanks. This was to be a common arrangement on future 2nd Armored tanks throughout the war years.

A closer look at the jerry can arrangement on the rear of another M2A4.
(Young Collection)

Bivouac Security

In hostile territory, any tank platoon or company lacking close ground troop support would circle the tanks like a covered wagon train in the Old West, taking advantage of terrain features. Within an outer ring would be placed an inner ring covering the intervals. Dismounted machine guns on tripods would fill any gaps and be sighted for criss-crossed lanes of fire, selected before dark. Any headquarters, maintenance and supply vehicles were inside these defenses.

In long halts for rest or sleep you might be safer in a slit trench than in a tank, which is such a large target. The personal safety of all individuals was not only derived from, but contributed to, the security and success of the entire team. This mutual benefit extended to every higher unit and echelon. In defence, as in offence, there could be no weak links.

Above: The maneuvers come to a close. Preparing the tanks for the return trip to Ft. Benning.

Below: Sgt. Joe Young wearing zipper style overalls and improved tanker's helmet. (Young Collection)

Above: Lining the tanks up for rail shipment. Cowan, Tennessee.

Below: Loading the tanks on flatcars for the trip back to Ft. Benning.

Chapter 3

Louisiana Maneuvers - August/September, 1941

Huge forces were involved, using over 13 million acres of Louisiana and part of east Texas. The Blitzkrieg tactics developed in Tennessee were to be polished in Louisiana. We were now the HELL ON WHEELS division. We saw Patton as the great star among the 400,000 soldiers in Louisiana and all of us, down to the lowliest private, **prayed with Patton at the altar of violent force and audacity**.

While high level strategy and tactics were being polished by the leaders, we had interesting problems in the lower echelons. Road march discipline was much more difficult than might appear in the photographs. Fifty yards had to be maintained between vehicles to avoid multiple hits from a single dropped bomb. The usual road march speed was 15 mph and if a vehicle slowed or speeded up a little, it could cause those following to over-react with speed changes and make the column telescope or expand like an accordion.

General Patton had learned to fly a small plane and it was his custom to fly over the maneuver area to check on movements of his units. On one occasion when a bunch of tanks were crowded up in a swampy area, a stream of profanity came down out of the sky, as Patton was flying over with a loudspeaker. The soldiers were cowed and the local citizens edified.

Dodge command car and Willys peep getting a rather wet and muddy start in the Louisiana Maneuvers.

Notice the long spacing between tanks during this simulated attack. In actual combat, a tank hit by a bomb or rocket could explode, taking other tanks with it if they were too near.

Simulated strafing by some of our newest dive bombers, said to be the world's best, reminded us that the AA machine guns on our turrets had a purpose. Some planes came danger-ously close and one of them knocked the top off of a pine tree with a wing tip, flying at 300-400 mph. The plane rocked but flew on.

A B-25 medium bomber flies overhead.

Above: Refueling tanks was always done with 5 gallon cans, individually emptied into the fuel tanks through the rear deck. This usually caused static electricity to ignite vapors, but fire and explosions were prevented by simply giving little squirts of the carbon dioxide fire extinguisher into the filler pipe. Notice the pioneer tool storage.

Below: An unfortunate M2A4 burns after catching fire. (Stalker Collection)

Above:
Spectacular slit trench view of an M3 Stuart during Louisiana Maneuvers, Sept., 1941. At first glance, it's easy to mistake an M3 for an M2A4 or vice versa. But on closer inspection, the M3 is distinguished from the M2A4 by the absence of the main gun recoil housing , covers over the turret vision slots and large idler wheel which contacts more of the track with the ground.
(Young Collection)

Below:
Driver in his M3 Stuart with the hatches completely opened. Whenever the situation allowed, opened driver and bow machine gunner hatches afforded excellent visibility.
(Young Collection)

The marshy areas were not always as obvious as one might hope. A M3 Stuart (left) and M2A4 have become victims to what looked like firm ground.

Louisiana Maneuvers Compared With Tennessee

The Louisiana swamps gave us a lot of practice in extracting tanks when stuck in soft ground. The deceptively firm crust could break through into much softer soil, called gumbo. Usually other tanks could pull out a stuck tank. The standard tow cables on each tank were absolutely essential.

Unlike frequent long road marches and encirclements in Tennessee, in Louisiana we were forced to operate in narrow quarters between great boggy areas, sometimes covering only a few miles of front with a whole tank regiment.

We were surprised at the realism of simulated combat between units of all sizes. Movement and action, coordination of effort, excitement, noise, hunger and exhaustion approximated the real thing. The firing of large and small weapon blank ammunition could scarcely be heard above the roar, clatter and rumble of armored vehicles.

Giant Army sound trucks off in the forests broadcast amplified recordings of bombs, sirens, cannon fire, rifle and machine gun fire, the hissing of gas canisters and the roar of airplanes and motors. This added realism was so loud that we had to shout to be heard. The presence of burned powder, diesel exhaust, smoke and dust left nothing to add. The news writers and photographers were having a field day.

Many Louisiana natives got a thrill as an armored column would thunder through a town, shaking windows and awakening the residents, with tanks weighing from 8 to 28 tons, scout cars, jeeps, wreckers, big guns and caissons, heavy trucks and motorcycles. Our tanks tore up roads dreadfully, broke through bridges and put huge ripples in blacktop paving, like the waves behind a steamboat. We knocked down trees and fences, destroyed crops and made new roads and hasty bridges when needed. On one exercise, 3,000 vehicles and 11,000 men got through a big mess in about 15 hours without leaving behind a single vehicle, a remarkable feat.

Above:
A Co. H tank added to the list of delays.

(Young Collection)

Left:
An F Co. tank helplessly stuck in the gumbo.

The Incident Of The Misfired 75 mm Cannon

When Co. H, 66th, was attacking anti-tank gun positions, one of the guns fired a blank at my tank at about 200 yards. The gun hung fire but went off when we were just a few yards from it. With our driver and bow gunner doors open for better vision and safety to ground troops, the blast entered the front of the tank so violently that we would have been injured if we had not been wearing goggles, dust masks and helmets. We were furious because we thought it had been a deliberate shot at close range. I let my driver charge the gun, running over the trails and leaving it pointing up at a useless angle. I had to restrain him from chasing the artillery crew. The others in the company promptly dubbed the driver "Killer". The picture of those pale, bug-eyed artillery men did wonders for Co. H. morale.

Above:
Model M1897A 75 mm field gun of the 14th Field Artillery ready for action.

Below:
Manhandling a 75 mm field gun into position. The M1897A 75 mm field gun was an American variant of a French design used in World War I. By late 1941, the gun would be mounted on M3 GMC halftracks (75 mm Gun Motor Carriage M3) and used by American troops in the Phillipines against the Japanese. Later, in Tunisia, North Africa, they would be used against the Germans. The British also used the 75 mm Gun Motor Carriage M3, re-designating it "75 mm SP, Autocar" (Autocar being the manufacturer).

"The charge that failed", Peason Ridge, Louisiana. (Stalker Collection)

In these maneuvers the delay and vulnerability of a stuck tank was considered a serious matter. Not only could a crew and tank be lost but a platoon could fail, and so on up the chain, to company and battalion. A stuck tank could be a disgrace and shame in training but a disaster in combat. The whole concept of the welfare of the team was the source of many later selfless acts of individual heroism.

Jumping a dismantled bridge.

Jumping A Dismantled Bridge

In a jeep, I was making a reconnaissance for my company commander in a pine forest. We must have been behind the enemy lines because as we went down a forest road, a halftrack on a side lane pulled out behind us, blocking our return. A couple of hundred yards ahead we found a small bridge with each ramp intact but the bridge bed proper lacking several planks which had been removed and neatly piled beside the road. The planks were 3 x 12 inches, on about a 15 foot ramp on each side of the vacant center of the bridge. I backed up perhaps a hundred yards, believing that if the Marines with a towed 37 mm gun could jump, as illustrated in one of their recruiting advertisements, with all six wheels off the ground, I could do the same without a towed gun.

With my heart in my mouth, I hit the near bridge ramp at about 55 mph, with the car in 4-wheel drive and my foot on the throttle for better control. We struck the ramp with a loud bang and jumped all the way across the bridge, including the opposite ramp, and landed on the road beyond with a tremendous wham, the front wheels coming down first. The jeep suffered no ill effects but it took us 12 miles of exploring to find our way back to the company.

Co. H tank crews rebuilding a damaged bridge.

Repairing A Broken Bridge

We were very proud of an episode in east Texas. Part of the division had crossed the Sabine River in southern Louisiana to make a long end run to envelop Shreveport in northern Louisiana. My tank almost fell through a breaking 16-foot section of a wooden bridge across a very wide swamp. We just barely teetered up onto the next section of the bridge. Then word was passed forward to us that the company following us had broken a bridge to our rear, so we were trapped. Using our pioneer tools, we cut several logs from a nearby island to which we had waded and floated them over to the broken bridge. We had to stomp on water moccasin snakes as we carried the logs off the island. We used the logs to replace the broken joists, anchoring them at one end only, to allow for sagging. We replaced all the planks and gingerly drove the rest of the tank company across the repaired section.

This end run through western Louisiana and east Texas was the longest and most completely self sustaining maneuver ever made by a large force in a short time. The entire division moved 186 miles in a day and a night. This was a tactical move with complete reconnaissance and flank protection all the way. The latter had to go through river bottoms, swamps, semi-jungles and countless side roads in Texas, at great speed and effort to keep up with the main force. It was a feat never before attempted or thought possible by a large armored unit.

An exhausted crew taking a short nap during one of the all too few breaks during the Louisiana Maneuvers.

Breaking The Rules

Patton made his own rules in taking a long detour out of the maneuver area and paying cash for large amounts of fuel from civilian sources. His actions won the war game and ended it a whole day ahead of schedule. We washed the mud out of our shoes and put them back on over dry socks.

During one maneuver in Louisiana a newly graduated West Point 2nd Lieutenant disobeyed direct orders by taking a 2-1/2 ton maintenance truck across our route after an order had been given to retreat. It mired down hopelessly after slipping off of a bridge, and we were in danger of losing a battalion of tanks trapped beyond it if we spent time to pull the truck out. In the dark, no one but my company and the truck crew knew what had occurred. To save the lieutenant's career and to clear the road, we yanked the truck over on its side with a tank and covered it with brush so that no one else would notice it. After our tank column had withdrawn past it, we hooked our four last tanks onto the truck from different angles, dragged it up over a mass of broken timbers and mud, set it up on its wheels, refilled its crankcase with oil and sent it on its way, to the tremendous relief of that new lieutenant.

Above: An M2A1 medium tank of the 67th Armored Regiment moving at top speed. By mid 1941, the M2A1 represented a design quickly becoming obsolete. This vehicle is displaying a prewar insignia (star on a blue shield with a red dot), and white cross wargame recognition markings. The M2A1's maximum armor thickness was 32 mm.

Below: "Men from Mars." Tankers try on their compact gas masks. These were later taken overseas as a precautionary measure.

Left:
One of the motorcycles used by Co. H runners.

Below:
The Louisiana Maneuvers had it's share of accidents also. Here, tankers and an ambulance driver aid a hapless motorcycle rider with a broken leg into a Dodge T212 ambulance. Notice the jerry can arrangement on both fenders of the M3 and the tools.

Above: A Dodge supply truck has rolled on its side in Alabama, due to a faulty steering mechanism.

Below: Peep given a checkup after 1000 miles.

Above: M3 Stuart with welded and riveted turret. The M3 Stuart's maximum armor thickness was 31 mm.

Below: Complete M3 Stuart crew.

Above: Battalion Commander, Maj. Mitchell standing in front of his command M2 halftrack.

Below: Regimental command post. The cloth hats were an indication of a rest area.

Above: Removing debris from the suspension of an M3 Stuart. (U.S. Army)

Below: 2nd Armored Division staff headquarters during the Louisiana maneuvers. (Stalker Collection)

Above: Crossing the Mississippi on the train back to Ft. Benning. Below: Traveling through the state of Mississippi.

Termination Of The Louisiana Maneuvers

Leaving Louisiana, we had to make a 223 mile non-tactical road march across the state to the entraining point. This was an all-time record for time and distance. The column was 110 miles long and took 7 hours to go through towns along the way. We had never tasted such good black coffee in the middle of the night.

Chapter 4

Carolina Maneuvers - November, 1941
With Diesel Tanks

Our 420 mile march to the maneuver area was the largest vehicular movement in the history of any American division. 2,500 vehicles went by road, while the tracked vehicles went by train. The division did have some of the new M3 General Grant medium tanks, but we had not as yet been reorganized and were using a newer light tank. These were the 14 ton M2A4 diesel tanks, a variant which was more powerful, faster, had better armor and a more stable suspension system than previous models.

The Guiberson T1020, a 9 cylinder air cooled radial diesel engine, was the most powerful engine for its weight in existence and there was much less danger of fire. However, it proved to be impractical because of the difficulty of starting in cold weather. The engine had to be hand cranked just past dead center compression on one cylinder and a blank shotgun shell fired from a chamber inside the hull, the pressure going through a pipe into the cylinder to kick the engine over 6 or 7 revolutions. If several shells failed to start the engine, we usually got another tank that was running to tow it off. On some cold mornings in the Carolinas we had to use 3 or 4 tanks to tow off all the rest of the company. Also, we had to be very careful not to put diesel fuel in cans that had held gasoline, because the enriched mixture could blow the head off of a cylinder. The nine little fuel injector piston assemblies had only 5 millionths of an inch tolerance and our mechanics always had to handle them in oil, because touching them dry with bare fingers would ruin them.

A dusty road march through North Carolina.

Above: Early production diesel M3 Stuarts, an M2 halftrack and Willys jeep prepare to move out. The Willys peep was now called jeep as it had totally replaced the Dodge command car. Chester, South Carolina.

Below: Preparing a delaying action at Sturdevant's Crossroad, North Carolina. The Russians had recently used this tactic against the Germans and the U.S. Army emulated it.

Radios

When we still had the diesel tanks we got our first modern FM radios, in South Carolina. The associated intercom finally obviated the need for foot signals to the drivers. Eventually, the division received 600 FM radios.

I got my break in the Carolina maneuvers when my company commander, acting as gunner in his tank, turned his 37 mm cannon to one side while going down a steep hill in a pine forest. A tree struck the gun barrel, spun the turret around two complete revolutions as it tore up the cog wheels, dislocated the captain's shoulder and banged him up considerably, putting him in the hospital. I became company commander and grew a moustache.

Above:
M2 command halftrack caught at a lull during the Carolina Maneuvers. Notice the canvas top, jerry can arrangement, and white wargame recognition circle.
(Young Collection)

Left:
M3 Stuart negotiating a small ford. The Carolina Maneuvers would see the demise of the M2A4 as a front line tank for the U.S. Army. It was being completely replaced by the M3 Stuart. During the war years the M2A4 would be relegated to training units. The M2A4 was released to the U.S. Marines where it saw limited combat in the Pacific. The British also received the M2A4 and used them in Libya though they did not see action.

Bulldozer blazing a road through the wilderness. Notice that no time is being wasted; a tank follows close behind.

Prelude To The Battle Of Cheraw, South Carolina

A large "enemy" force had crossed into our territory. The First and Second Armored Divisions made a frontal attack while our 66th Armored Regiment, with the help of engineers, armored cars and light artillery, forced its way through a veritable jungle down in bottom land alongside the Pee Dee River, getting within artillery range of two bridges. Two tank companies of our battalion and a company of engineers wormed their way through the bewildering jungle of trees and vines for 4 or 5 miles. The photographs show the early stages of this as dusk fell. Within two hours, this pioneered path was a roaring, throbbing boulevard of bulldozers, tanks, light and heavy artillery, anti-aircraft guns, armored cars, armored personnel carriers,

kitchens, supply trucks, wreckers and maintenance crews. Destruction of the bridge cut off an entire enemy division without supplies and we then turned directly into Cheraw.

We were now at the enemy's rear and had a running engagement across the outskirts of Cheraw, with mobile artillery firing blanks and laying down real smoke screens. Since it was getting dark it was easy to see flares dropped from airplanes. Our new radios helped in assembling the various units.

A large "enemy" force then moved in to cut us off. Our whole armored corps was withdrawn in a complex blackout march, during

which one of our light tanks rolled 50 feet down a steep bank into a rock quarry. The platoon sergeant radioed "no injuries whatsoever, antenna slightly bent, tank upside down." When a tank rolled over, it was standard procedure for the commander to pull in his head and the gunner to hug the gun and shoulder guard and roll with it. All crew members routinely wore safety belts. Two nights later, we sneaked a wrecker truck back, righted the tank and sent it on its way. I think we company grade officers and men had more fun than the colonels and generals.

Above:
M2 halftracks traveling on their newly acquired road. The company maintenance sergeant is in H-2.

Left:
Artillery support brings up the rear as night falls.

The M1A1 90 mm gun set and ready for action. The loader has placed a round in the auto rammer. This gun system was "state of the art" for 1941 and was only 6 months old when this photo was taken.

Capturing An Anti-Aircraft Battery

On one maneuver, Co. H tanks, with the command halftrack, went through a few miles of dense pine forest and rough country, crossing streams and gullies. We were excited to discover through an opening in the trees an anti-aircraft battery set up on an open hillside ahead of us. Our final approach to this was uphill through the trees, running slowly and quietly with our engines in low gear. We then burst out of the edge of the woods in a line of several tanks at top speed, catching the artillery battery completely by surprise. They were bivouacked in a cemetery and, as we circled around through the cemetery and surrounded the guns, mess kits and half-eaten meals were thrown all over the place. It was total shock action and surprise. The local umpire was junior to the lieutenant-colonel in command of the battery, presumably both concerned about their careers and future promotions, and the umpire decided that we had lost the engagement!

Anti-aircraft personel checking the direction system for the 90 mm gun.

In the mid-thirties it became apparent that the 3 inch AA (anti-aircraft) guns then in service were quickly becoming inadequate. Therefore, in 1938 the Coastal Artillery Board, being responsible for AA equipment, requested a proper replacement with improved qualities be designed. It was imperative the AA gun be able to fire a shell no lighter than 21 lbs but needed to be hand loaded. By March 1940, the 90 mm M1 was tested and approved for service. The gun was of conventional design with a vertical sliding breech block. It was mounted on a four-outrigger platform and used two single axles with double wheels. One of the outriggers was fixed and used for a towing bar while the other three outriggers could be folded up for transport.

By May 1941, several improvements were incorporated into the M1, creating the M1A1. The M1A1 improvements included a fuse setter, spring actuated auto power rammer to speed the rate of fire to 28 rounds per minute, and remote power to the gun from the director (see photo above).

By 1942, over 2000 M1A1s had been produced. The M1A1 was the standard AA gun of U.S. forces and was used in every theater of the war, including London. For all its merits, it was still considered inferior to the German 88 mm flak gun.

Exhausted crewmen take a deserved nap during the arduous road marches across the Carolinas.

Sleeping On Campaign

When there wasn't time for a bivouac (by definition, a temporary encampment without shelter), we slept on the ground. You couldn't lie down in a light tank so you found a place between trees where you would not get run over. In the bitter cold and wet weather of the Carolinas, we managed to be quite snug in our heavy canvas bedrolls which were water resistant. By the time you wriggled into it, fully dressed, with several layers of clothing and boots, the bedroll became a round tube which would roll on a hillside. The heavy zippers worked pretty well until clogged with mud.

War correspondents have commented on how quickly a resting soldier can go to sleep. This is based not only on mental and physical fatigue but on the security and equanimity of being part of a well trained team.

Left:
A 78th Field Artillery halftrack negotiates a hastily built road.

Below:
M3 Stuarts attacking in a wedge formation. Before the advent of FM radios in November, 1941, formations were controlled by arm or flag signals. This platoon has an extra tank; at this time, March 25, 1942, light tank companies had 13 tanks, with only 4 per platoon. (U.S. Army)

Wedge Formation
(1) Affords good fire power to the front and each flank.
(2) Provides good directional control, but the control depends largely upon visual contact between adjacent tanks.
(3) Lends itself readily to development of movement by bounds of fire and maneuver.
(4) Is used prior to contact when the platoon leader wants to maintain maximum control though deployed.

Above & Below: Assembling after the Carolina maneuvers. Cheraw, South Carolina.

Chapter 5

Pearl Harbor And Ft. Benning

Pearl Harbor, December 7, 1941 occurred when we were receiving new M3 General Grant medium tanks. The initial shock of Pearl Harbor was soon replaced with a feeling of relief, for now we knew what we had been training for. Although all lives were being changed, with a sense of real loss for some, a happier and more confident mood began to prevail, stimulated by the knowledge of what was expected of us, by the sound of the National Anthem, stories of heroism in the Pacific and the flowing surge of power across the country.

Extensive reorganization of the division re-

sulted from maneuver experiences and the expected needs of the war. The tank brigade was too unwieldy, so it was split into two Combat Commands, each with one tank regiment and any other units attached to fit the situation. The result was greater flexibility.

The 68th Armored Regiment was deactivated and divided up between the 66th and 67th, which each then had two medium tank battalions and one light tank battalion. Incidentally, the light tank battalions had been exchanging their M2A4s for M3 light tanks which had a larger rear idler, increasing ground contact. The Brit-

Unmistakably pleased recipients of new Chrysler produced M3 Grant medium tanks. The Sam Browne belts were relics of when they were needed to support the weight of a saber and scabbard.

Lady tanker poses next to her date. On this occasion, tankers took their girl friends for a drive in their new M3 Grants. The ladies were afforded what few women had the opportunity to do, drive a tank.

ish were using the M3s in Libya against the Germans and called them "Honeys". By early 1942, the new 16-1/2 ton M5 light tank was in use, powered by twin Cadillac V-8 engines.

The Ordnance and Quartermaster battalions had their names changed to Maintenance and Supply and, along with the Medical Battalion were in the Division Trains. The Reconnaisance Battalion lost its infantry company and gained a light tank company. The Engineer Battalion acquired new treadway bridges which could take any vehicle from tanks to motorcycles. The artillery was now all under a single command, with several changes in unit names, and could be parcelled out to the Combat Commands.

These changes required arduous effort by all ranks. Old equipment was turned in or exchanged, shortages corrected and new equipment accepted. This required exhaustive inventories of everything from tanks and their contents to kitchen pans. The work of the 2500 men in our regiment had to be tallied in day-and-night-

long meetings of scores of men and officers at the regimental level.

A company commander is financially accountable and liable for every item in his company from tanks to pistols. I couldn't find the right officer to sign for my old tanks so I am still waiting for some clerk in the hidden recesses of an army records building to have me billed for 13 light tanks. This is not entirely a joke; I met a senior officer in 1940 who was being billed a ruinous sum for equipment he had failed to account for in World War I!

Even more complex were training schedules during this period of urgency. On a single day in our company alone, non-coms might be conducting ten different classes of instruction, for example, in weapons firing, maintenance, radios, map reading, military intelligence, vehicle driving, defence for the disarmed soldier and use of handgrenades. Each day was different because new recruits were in different stages of training.

An M3 Grant crew watching troops of the 4th Division march by during maneuvers at Ft. Benning. Notice the unit marking on the three piece final drive housing.

The M3 General Grant

Our company organization changed from 13 light tanks to 17 medium tanks per company, with two tanks in the company headquarters and five tanks in each of three platoons. We were thrilled at first with the Chrysler-built M3 General Grant tanks. But they were ungainly beasts, 18-1/2 feet long and 13 feet tall with the cupola covers open and the .50 caliber anti-aircraft machine gun mounted. With the top hatch closed and the gun stowed, the tank was still 10 feet 3 inches tall. The M3 required a six-man crew of tank commander, driver, two gunners and two loaders. Our Maintenance Sergeant said it looked like a "damned cathedral coming down the road".

The 75 mm cannon in the sponson in the right hull would traverse only 30 degrees. A 37 mm cannon, with a coaxial machine gun, in the fully rotating turret, was flexible and fast but not much good against modern armor. The turret was offset a little to the left, to balance the 75 mm on the right. There were gyro-stabilizers for both cannons, ostensibly allowing them to fire while in motion.

The total weight of the M3 was 28-30 tons, with maximum armor thickness of 57 mm. These tanks were more difficult to handle than the light tanks and one track was more likely to sink in soft ground. Sometimes a heavy maintenance truck with a winch and cable could tilt the tank away from the sunken side to aid in restoring a thrown track.

Lt. Perkins in tanker's suit and helmet poses next to a new M3 Grant.

Driving a tank was easy to learn on roads or hard ground. We had tank drivers who had never learned to drive an automobile. My future wife, on our third date, drove an M3 Grant five miles in a training area at Ft. Benning in Februaby, 1942. The tanks were all steered or braked with steering brake levers, while the clutch, the 5-speed stick shift and throttle were as in an automobile. A hand throttle could be set for cruising on the highway. The M3 Grant had a top speed of 26 mph.

In the M3 we had two cannons to boresight instead of one. Cross hairs were taped in slots on the muzzles. The gunner then lined them up on a distant aiming point while looking through a breech boresight or through the firing pin hole with the breech closed. He then adjusted the gun sight on the same target point.

Above: Co. H Grants lined up for inspection.

Below: Ft. Benning. This photo shows a portion of the cantonment area used by the Second Armored Division for two years. (Stalker Collection)

This unfortunate tank has discovered the soft marshy ground of Ft. Benning. Notice the M1 Ward La-France wrecker in the background.

Swamp Trouble At Ft. Benning

On February 17, 1942, my company of Grant tanks was to lead a rehearsal of our entire battalion for a demonstration of a combined arms attack in an area 3/4 mile by 1-1/2 miles of little hills, trees, streams and trails. It was a disaster. Twenty tanks immediately got stuck, even though on the best available ground, because it had been made spongy by freezing and winter rains. The top brass had failed to make an adequate reconnaissance. The demonstration was called off but the stuck tanks blocked the routes of all the others. Meals were to be sent out to us in light vehicles while we were waiting for the engineers, because it was deemed impossible to get any of the tanks out by nightfall.

Co. H was not satisfied with this and we discovered the ground was harder under standing water. We took a chance and sent two tanks off through a swamp, going close to trees to take advantage of their roots. One tank soon sank in the gumbo, a hundred yards from any ground hard enough for another tank to pull from. We cut down trees and developed a spe-

cial way of laying in log cribs so the tank could lift itself out. In half an hour we had it back with the others. Meanwhile, the other tank had gone a few hundred yards before getting stuck. We decided to get the most out of the experience and organized the company into crews working in relays with our pioneer tools (axes and shovels). We cut about 80 pine trees, chopped them up in short lengths and built cradles, bridges and matting. In three hours we took the 28 ton brute 1,000 yards to hard ground. It was fun to watch it sink a carefully built corduroy road about three feet and then pull itself out anyway.

We used a dirt road part way and got a good impression of the weight of 28 tons when parts of the road sank two feet while the ground we were standing on beside it bulged up. We found another way out for the rest of our company and got home before dark. The unfortunate remainder of the battalion had to follow in the morass we left and didn't get home until all hours of the night. It was a very instructive experience in never-say-die teamwork.

Above: Grant crews quickly discovered the navigational differences of their mediums as compared to their previous light tanks.

Below: M1 Ward LaFrance wrecker pulls the Grant up on its side, freeing it from the sticky "gumbo".

M3 Grants under shelter. Notice the large unit markings on the differential housings. (Stalker Collection)

Shooting At Our Own Tanks With Live Ammunition

In a field exercise in March, 1942, three supporting Grant crews, in firing positions, impulsively began firing machine guns at two other tanks which were charging the objective. They were buttoned up so that there was virtually no danger to the crews. Hearing the bullets striking the hull, they joined in the spirit of the fun and began dodging and zig zagging, giving the supporting tanks some excellent practice in shooting at moving targets with tracers. This was unauthorized, and if any periscopes were damaged, it wasn't reported.

It was in March, 1942, that we named each individual vehicle, using the company designation as the initial letter of each name. Many crews kept the same names, even on replacement tanks, through the African and European campaigns. In H/66, the command tank was *Hannibal*; staff tank, *Honeychile*; platoon tanks, *Hungunner*, *Hurricane*, *Holy Joe*, *Hotspur*, *Hotshot*, *Hazard*, *Havoc*, *Hypo*, *Hawkeye*, *Houdini*, *Hellcat*, *Haymaker*, *Hangover*, *Hornet*, *Halleluiah*; T2 tank retriever, *Hardup*; command halftrack, *Harrier*.

28 ton Grant tank crossing a 6 ton bridge.

Gasoline Fire In An M3 Grant Tank

This tank was sitting on the edge of a road on maneuvers, tilted and failed to start. We got one of the maintenance crew to see what he could do. While he was sitting in the driver's seat, the tilt caused a full gas tank to leak, overflowing through the filler cap. Some of the gasoline seeped into the fighting compartment and vaporized. The mechanic stepped on the starter, a spark ignited the fumes, and a seething mass of red flames came out of the hatch in the right side sponson. Two of us rushed to the hatch, wondering if we were going to have to be heroes and go in and get the guy. Fortunately he crawled out, whimpering and groaning, with the skin falling off of his face and his wrists. Other crews ran up with fire extinguishers and put out the fire. The mechanic was Sergeant Childers, who had only 2nd degree burns. He healed, came back to the company, and finished the war known as Pinkey because the skin never grew back tan again.

Gathering of tankers during a combat exercise critique. They are wearing clothing and gear more characteristic of the World War II tankers.

Forbidden Fun In Phenix

The unfettered Second Armored fighting spirit regularly found expression during weekend passes in Columbus or across the Chattahoochee in Phenix City, Alabama. It became a point of honor and almost a ritual to challenge and fight the paratroopers of the 82nd Airborne. These forays found their consummation outside dance halls, bordellos and bars. Heaven help the M.P.s when payday came on Saturday!

Split scalps, broken hands and bottle cuts were the battle stripes from these off-the-post proving grounds. We knew who the fighters were by the gleam in their eyes as they left for the battle zone. We neither condoned nor condemned this form of "training". Who wants to deny a soldier of his off-duty fun?

Chapter 6

North Carolina Maneuvers and Ft. Bragg, 1942

We went back to the Carolinas again in July, 1942. The mood of urgency in the training and reorganization which characterized the division at Ft. Benning after Pearl Harbor was evolving into a growing confidence in our readiness and eagerness to prove ourselves in battle. By now we were old hands at adapting to change and were delighted with the new equipment, including the new light weight all-vehicle pontoon bridges. And with knowledge of the faults of the ungainly M3 Grants, we were soon to jump into the more flexible and efficient M4's with great satisfaction.

There also was less tension now that we were more removed from the gossip mills, jealousies and anxieties of Ft. Benning and their effect on our professional efficiency. Shedding those stresses and being preoccupied with our coming missions fostered a new equanimity. Many wives followed us to the vicinity of Ft. Bragg, but family separations were beginning.

Responding to the apparent uncertainty in the War Dept. as to where our division would be employed, we soaked up every rumor about whether we would go to the Pacific ot to Europe. Whatever befell us, we expected it would be fullfilling to our men and machines.

M3 Grants lead a column of vehicles across a flexible, lightweight pontoon bridge spanning the Pee Dee River, South Carolina.

Above: M2 and M3 halftracks cross the pontoon bridge .

Below: Command halftrack with radio, an SCR 510. The powerful .50 cal. machine gun shown was becoming more common, supported in this vehicle by two older .30 cal. machine guns.

Left:
M3 Grant crosses a pontoon bridge.

Below:
A 75 mm Howitzer Motor Carriage T30 during maneuvers at Ft. Benning in July 1942. The T30 was created when two M3 GMC halftracks were fitted with M1A1 75 mm howitzers. These prototypes were produced by the Ordnance Dept. in Jan. 1942 and after successful testing, an order was placed for 500 vehicles. The T30 was used by medium tank HQ units. It was considered a "stopgap" measure, and was replaced by the 75 mm Howitzer Motor Carriage M8 in 1943.

Above: From left to right; Lt. Bakey, Capt. Perkins and Lt. Fleet study a rainproof map pack.

Below: Taking a well deserved break next to their command halftrack, "HARRIER".

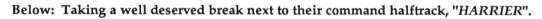

Second Armored receives its new Sherman tanks. These are early production M4A1 tanks produced by Pacific Car & Foundry. Notice the turret tops have been painted white. The two Shermans most prominent in the photo have three piece final drive housings and the tank on the left has direct vision slots while the tank on the right has periscopes. These subtle variations are but a few common to the Sherman.

The M4 General Sherman Tank

Finally we got into our main battle tank for World War II when we were in a semi-staging area at Ft. Bragg. The Sherman, costing $60,000, was 9 feet high, buttoned up, or 10-1/2 feet high with hatches open and turret anti-aircraft gun mounted. It was 19 feet 4 inches long and 8 feet 7 inches wide. Armor thickness was 75 mm in the front of the turret and 50 mm in the front slope plate of the hull. Maximum speed was officially 24-29 mph. It could cross a 7 foot 5 inch trench. Over 40,000 Shermans were built in World War II for the U.S. and Allies. Several different engines were used, depending on what was available.

Our Shermans at that time were provided with a converted Wright Whirlwind, 9 cylinder, air-cooled, radial aircraft engine of around 400 horsepower, costing $5,000. The set of tools for its maintenance cost $8,000. The engine and fuel tanks were in the rear. This engine had to be pulled in order to change all the spark plugs and we pulled it anyway every 100 hours for in-

spections and maintenance. By now, the tanks and all other vehicles in the division used the same 84 octane gasoline. The Sherman's four fuel tanks carried 185 gallons of gasoline which, off the highway, would take it 45-90 miles, at 1/4 to 1/2 mile per gallon.

The tank driver had to watch and control the temperature, oil pressure, gear ratio, engine speed by tachometer, generator output, amperage and voltage, and observe several precautions when starting and stopping the engine. He was an expert in field expedients and field repairs. Because all five crew members had to learn all five positions including gunnery and radio operation, we became pretty proud of this knowledge and expertise. We believed that a thoroughly trained tank driver had a more complex job than an airplane pilot. Tank drivers often, in campaigns, were promoted to tank commander where they also had to be map readers, tacticians and leaders.

Above:
M4A1 Shermans during inspection. This particular tank has a one piece final drive housing.

Left:
Early M4A1 with direct vision slots. This vehicle has a one piece final drive housing.

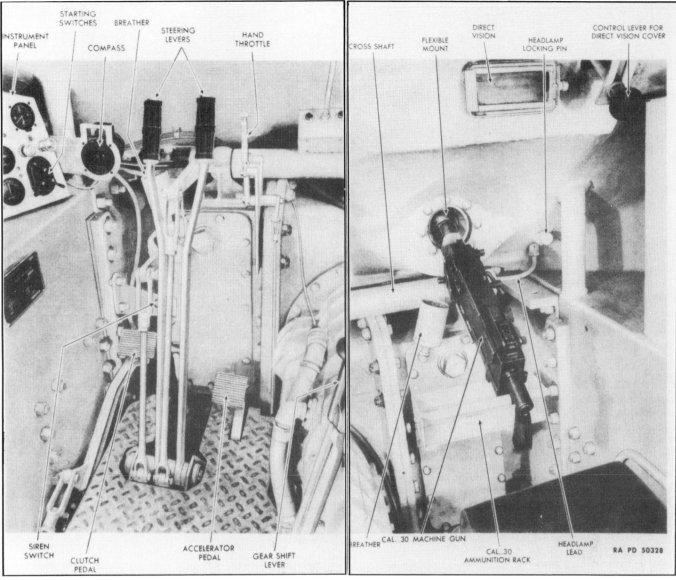

Interior view of the driver's controls in an M4. (TM 9-731A)

Interior view of the assistant driver's station in the right bow. (TM 9-731A)

The Sherman Crew

The tank commander could stand or sit up in a cupola in the right side of the large turret; the corporal gunner, in a seat in front of him, sat to the right of the breech of the cannon and the loader-radio operator sat or stood in the left side of the turret. The driver, down in the hull, was on the left, the bow gunner on the right. All eventually had periscopes. The commander's, driver's and bow gunner's 'scopes were in their hatch covers, while the gunner's was his gun-sight, with a reticle for aiming and ranging. It was possible to look through a periscope with field glasses.

Standard production M4A1.

Claustrophobia

A tank was no place for a person with claustrophobia. We had one man in the company by the name of Smith who wet his pants every time he got in the tank and, of course, we had to transfer him out. We called him "Pissing Smith".

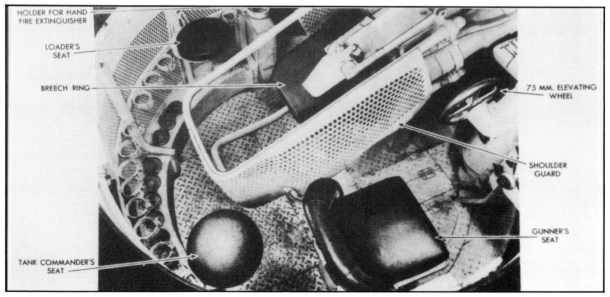

Interior view of the turret fighting compartment. (TM 9-731A)

On 8 January 1942, Following its reorganization after the first Carolina maneuvers, the Division had been constituted as follows:

Second Armored Division

Commanded by Major General George S. Patton, Jr.

Division Headquarters and Headquarters Company:
    Headquarters Combat Command "A"
    Headquarters Combat Command "B"

Division Service Company

142nd Armored Signal Company (Formerly 48th Signal Company)

Division Artillery Headquarters
    14th Armored Field Artillery Battalion
    78th Armored Field Artillery
    92nd Armored Field Artillery Battalion

Division Trains Headquarters and Headquarters Company:
    48th Armored Medical Battalion
    2nd Armored Maintenance Battalion (Formerly 17th Ordnance Battalion)
    2nd Armored Supply Battalion (Formerly 14th Quartermaster Battalion)

66th Armored Regiment

67th Armored Regiment

41st Armored Infantry Regiment

17th Armored Engineer Battalion

82d Armored Reconnaissance Battalion (Formerly 2d Reconnaissance Battalion)

Another Gasoline Accident

One of our Sherman tanks was sitting in the tank park at Ft. Bragg, being refueled and undergoing routine inspection. Gasoline being poured into the fuel tanks partially vaporized and the explosive vapor was sucked down into the turret and fighting compartment by a gentle breeze. When the driver checked his siren switch there apparently was an arc which ignited the vapors. This was such a great explosion that it ripped off a metal-mounted rubber pad from the inside of the turret hatch and bent down the floor of the turret. The driver's helmet was blown straight up in the air through his open hatch but, because he was sitting almost in the center of the blast, with everything going away from him, his only injury was mild burns of the face and exposed parts of his wrists and ankles. Within seconds other tank crews had rushed up with fire extinguishers and put out the fire.

M4A2 with direct vision slots, welded hull and early suspension (track return rollers mounted over the tops of the bogie frames).

Weapons

A 75 mm cannon was the standard, but was being replaced by 76 mm during the European campaign. The coaxial .30 caliber machine gun was close to the cannon, as in the light tanks, both fired electrically with the gunner's foot switches. The bow .30 caliber machine gun, in a ball mount, was aimed by the bow gunner watching his tracers through his vision slot or, later, periscope. The anti-aircraft gun mounted outside the cupola was .50 caliber. A completely buttoned up Sherman allowed the commander to look through his periscope mounted in one of the hinged covers of his cupola, which he could rotate. The other half of the cupola cover could be left open so that he could stick his head out for a quick, more panoramic view. The commander had a toggle switch that would turn the turret 360 degrees in 15 seconds and a vertical sighting vane on the top of the turret as a crude aiming device for bringing a target into view of the gunner.

There was not a very bad noise level inside the tank. The cannon fire rocked the tank a little and was simply a big, heavy, satisfying "whump", unless you stuck your head out of the turret, in which case you had to be sure your ear flaps protected your ears. (Later in the war, the 90 mm muzzle blast rebound in the Pershing tank would suck the helmet right off of your head if you didn't have the chin strap fastened when your head was out of the turret. Also, when the breech block opened for the 90 mm during recoil, a tongue of flame and smoke would blow back into the turret, cleared by a strong blower in the fighting compartment.)

Early M4A1 with three piece final drive housing, and direct vision slots. This variant was supplied to the British who designated it Sherman II .

Stowage In The Sherman

In August, 1942 we were receiving an average of two new Shermans every day in Co. H and it took five men two days to check the equipment of each tank and stow it properly. The up-to-35-ton weight of the tank included 3,000 pounds of stowage. The following is a list, somewhat by category, of what went into or onto a Sherman tank. Most officers never did know where all of these things were stowed.

Ammunition:

90 rounds of 75 mm cannon shells; at least 8,000 rounds of belted .30 caliber machine gun shells; 300 rounds of belted .50 caliber; 600 rounds of .45 caliber for Tommy guns and pistols; 12 hand grenades and several smoke grenades, some colored.

Spare Tank Weapons:

Two additional air-cooled. .30 caliber machine guns with folding tripod ground-mounts, totalling five machine guns in all.

Individual Weapons:

A .45 automatic pistol for the commander, a couple of tommy guns, a Garand carbine and an M1 rifle.

Individual Equipment:

All crew members had the helmets previously described and all wore throat microphones attached, along with the ear phones, to the helmet cable; personal items in musette bags; goggles, dust masks, mess kits, canteens and compact short-term gas masks. The tank commander also had a map case, a small compass worn on his belt and a pair of field glasses. Coding and uncoding devices were kept in the company commander's tank.

Radios:

These were all push-button high frequency voice operated radios. The five command tanks (Company Commander's, his spare staff tank and the three platoon leader's) had the SCR (Signal Corps Radio) 508, a transmitter-two receiver set requiring two antennas. Six section leaders, two in each platoon, had the SCR 528, a trans-ceiver with one antenna. The remaining six tanks had the SCR 538, just a receiver. All of these radios were amplifiers for the intercoms. The radios were mounted in the rear turret bulge and could be quickly moved from tank to tank.

An extra radio, such as a CW long distance code set trans-ceiver, could be installed in the hull to the right of the bow gunner, requiring an extra antenna. Every tank had a hand microphone on a long cord in the turret.

Special Instruments:

A gunner's quadrant which could be placed on the cannon breech block to measure elevation was in every tank, for use in long-range indirect fire. Sometimes an artillery aiming circle was carried in a platoon leader's tank, but we didn't bother with them because we found a quicker expedient for paralleling guns. This will be discussed later.

Pioneer Tools:

These were usually kept in brackets on the outside of the tank, including sledges, shovels, axes and a pick-mattock. The tow cable was kept draped across the hull.

Miscellaneous Tank Equipment:

Asbestos mittens, folding canvas bucket, first aid kit and oil cans; canvas covers for periscopes, gun muzzles and exposed machine guns; flashlights, a signal flag, a recognition light, fire extinguishers; rammer staff and bore brushes for the cannon.

Spare Parts:

Track shoes, track connectors, lug nuts and bogey wheels were carried on the outside of the tank or in special compartments in the outer hull.

Inside were spare periscopes, gunsights, radio crystals, scores of machine gun parts, lamp bulbs and many tiny parts, even carburetor needle valves.

Tools:

Several kinds of wrenches, hammers, pliers, screw drivers, wire cutters, machine gun cleaning equipment and swabs.

Food:

A 3-day supply of C-ration cans (hash, vegetables and other foods) and D-ration bars (1,800 calories per bar which had to be eaten with water, a very hard chocolate compound).

Technical Manuals:

For the tank engine, all electrical systems, all weapons, the gyro-stabilizer, radios and even for the little gasoline auxiliary motor for charging the battery. A 396-page technical manual for the tank as a whole was kept in the maintenance section. Incidentally, the gasoline generator (Homelite brand) was a problem in the combat zone because the pop-popping of this little motor's exhaust could give away our position in a night bivouac or when we were trying to hide with the main engine off.

On the Outside:

Engine crank, rear hull. In addition to the pioneer tools, track parts and wheels, we carried a 12-foot square tarpaulin folded on the top of the back of the turret, a 45-foot square folded camouflage net on the back deck of the hull, and bedrolls in water resistant canvas bags. A spare supply of gasoline, oil, and water in five-gallon cans was carried in brackets on the back deck of the tank for long marches. Some of us kept a Bowie knife in a scabbard on the top of the turret in case needed to cut off burning luggage. The camouflage nets were very heavy and cumbersome because the 2-inch squares of net were laced with hundreds of feet of long, narrow strips of burlap. This, too, could catch fire from shell fragments. Grousers (track shoe attachments) were stored in compartments in the outer hull.

Pets:

I once found a tank crew in Louisiana with a tired armadillo walking around on the floor of the turret. That was a light tank. If we had had Shermans then I would have expected a small alligator, knowing our men.

The T2 Tank retriever was on an M3 Grant chassis and looked like a tank from the front, but the 75 and 37 mm guns were dummies and a strong derrick was on the back. Staff Sgt. McMahan, a tanker, was posed in this T2 by a Signal Corps photographer who thought it was a tank. (McMahan Collection)

The Maintenance Section

The 15-man maintenance crew with its T-2 tank retriever and two halftracks were commanded by a lieutenant, but the Maintenance Sergeant became one of the most important men in the company. The halftracks were virtual travelling repair shops, capable of serving a wide variety of repair functions in the combat zone, while the tank retriever could follow right into battle and save tanks from being total losses. Through training and experience, these 15 emergency mechanics were indispensable in heavy equipment and automotive repairs. They were revered by the tankers so dependent on machines for the consummation of their missions.

REAR SECTION-ENGINE
COMPARTMENT TOP PLATE

Removing the rear section of the engine compartment top plate.
(TM 9-731A)

Changing Motors In The Sherman

If we burned out a bearing, blew a cylinder head, got a leaky gasket or burned up a clutch, we could pull and replace the Wright Whirlwind engine very rapidly in the field. At Ft. Bragg, several miles from the main post one late afternoon, an engine blew a cylinder head and we radioed into the post to have our tank retriever bring out a spare engine. While waiting for the new engine, the tank crew unfastened the two top armor plates over the engine compartment, disconnected what they could reach of the power train; the electrical connections, exhaust, oil and fuel lines and all the controls and unbolted the engine. By then the tank retriever came out with it's derrick, lifted off the armor, pulled the engine out and dropped in the new engine. Soon it was all bolted in and hooked up. They were like a surgical team, working together with great coordination. The total elapsed time from beginning to open the engine compartment until the tank and engine were totally reassembled and running was 1-1/2 hours, which I never saw duplicated.

AIR INLET COVER

FORWARD SECTION-ENGINE
COMPARTMENT TOP PLATE

BAFFLE PLATE

RA

LIFTING SLING

SAFETY
CHAIN

Above left:
Pulling the forward section of the engine
compartment top plate. (TM 9-731A)

Above:
Lifting the engine from the M4 .
(TM 9-731A)

Left:
The engine partially lifted from the M4.
(TM 9-731A)

Dodge M6 Gun Motor Carriage and two Ford GPA amphibians.

An Assignment To The Deep Six

Supply Sergeant Tom Domarecki had a problem. He was too wise to burden the officers with it. On packing up for the move to the Ft. Dix, New Jersey, overseas staging area he assembled an excess of material which had no place in our tables of authorized equipment, no place to carry it and no documentation as to origins. There were two extra machine guns, several tools, sports equipment, other between-the-wars company fund property and a working air compressor. Nobody at Ft. Bragg would dare touch it. How would they be able to account for it? It is illegal to sell, give away or destroy usable Government property. Finding a solution in a maze of army regulations might take until World War III. So it all had to be stored somewhere, and in a hurry.

One day a committee of mourners in a 2-1/2 ton truck took three big boxes to a remote area on the reservation, dug a 6 ft. deep hole and planted the orphaned property. A marker cross was erected, with an envelope listing the contents of the boxes, but no names of relatives. One of the mourners, a religious former rum runner, spoke a few words over the grave. Other furtive parties were also in the woods too, pretending not to notice each other.

Rest assured, dear tax payers, nothing was destroyed. But there are no graveyard maps. Rest In Peace.

Chapter 7

The Invasion Of North Africa
November & December, 1942

Embarkation

The loading of the 3,000 vehicles and 15,000 men of the division in New York harbor was of such a complexity that few of us tankers had more than a small view of it. The first lift invaded North Africa in November, while our part of the division crossed the Atlantic in December.

Contemplate the delivery to the docks by railroad and the distribution to the cargo ships of tanks, tank destroyers, self-propelled artillery, towed guns, gun carriages, caissons, prime movers, weapons carriers, scout cars, halftracks, mortar carriers, recovery vehicles, wreckers, tank transporters, seven varieties of trucks, ammunition trailers, water tank trucks, cargo trailers, ambulances, field hospitals, motorcycles and jeeps. This list scarcely hints at the sub-specialized vehicles within those major headings.

Our own expert stowage of equipment inside of tanks was maddeningly redone and botched by officious quartermaster troops who were supposed to be helping us on the docks. All of this was further complicated by a longshoremen's strike.

Convoy To Morocco

Co H was lucky to be on the 528 foot long *Sea Train Texas*. Formerly a peace time carrier of railroad trains to Cuba, it now had the precious burden of 500 tanks and other vehicles, drawing 31 feet of water, in the center of the convoy, right behind the battleship *New York*. We had much freedom to be on deck, unlike some troop ships which carried as many as 5000 men. We had calisthenics on deck and did around-the-clock guard duty watching for submarines. A torpedo would have sunk this ship in 5 to 10 minutes, because it had no watertight compartments.

Training On The High Seas, Dec. 1942

We constructed, out of trash and cardboard, dummy traversing and elevating wheels, mounted on boxes, simulating the tank cannon controls. A target scene was painted on a canvas. The instructor drilled gunners in speedy adjustment of fire for pretended high or low shots, teaching rapid bracketing of targets. One of our platoon sergeants wrote from Europe in 1944 that this training in fast adjustment of fire had really paid off.

Several soldiers were killed when steel bunks broke loose on a big troop ship during a storm. We stood at attention on our little ship during the ceremony of delivering the bodies to the deep. Our protecting destroyers dropped a number of depth charges around the periphery of the convoy as we neared Morocco. In Casablanca our ship's on-board 90-ton derricks unloaded the tanks, tilting the ship as the tanks were swung over to the dock.

Twenty-eight months after it had been activated, the 2nd Armored Division had successfully made an amphibious assault landing on a hostile shore, the most difficult and dangerous of all operations.

Tanker with camouflaged head gear and Thompson sub machine gun.

Further Training In Morocco

After the successful 3-day campaign against the French in November, and further landings in December, intensive training was continued in the Cork Forest of Mamora north of Rabat, the capitol of French Morocco. We found that the 75 mm tank cannon was extremely accurate because of the excellent controls and heavy stability of the gun platform (the tank). As an example, we hit the trunk of a tree a mile away and knocked it down on the 3rd or 4th bracketing round. Even the .30 caliber ball-mounted bow gunner's machine gun, without any gunsight, was accurately controlled by watching the tracers through the periscope. He could roll a burst of fire into a hat at a couple of hundred yards.

A daring innovation by Lieutenant Colonel Harry Semmes was to have tanks close in on an objective all buttoned up while supporting artillery fired air burst shells directly over them. The air bursts would keep the enemy down with little risk of seriously damaging a tank. General Patton, Corps Commander, gleefully rode through one of these exercises in one of our tanks, firing the bow gun. The crew reported that he melted the machine gun barrel.

Although the cannon and the coaxial machine gun were gyro-stabilized so they would not pitch up and down as the tank encountered uneven ground in an assault, it was necessary to maintain a constant speed, because changing speed would cause the gun to hunt up and down.

We found that tank guns could be shot effectively from the deck of a rolling LCT (Landing Craft Tank). Gunners were taught to aim and fire at the top of a roll when the boat and the gun were momentarily motionless. It was also discovered that the projectile could be ricocheted off the water with the fuse set on delay so that an air burst could be achieved over the water or beach.

Improvisation was part of our life. For example, a tank platoon could be used like an artillery battery for indirect fire, but we simplified it. If we could find a distant aiming point that all tanks could lay on to parallel their guns we could dispense with dismounting and setting up an artllery aiming circle. All turret-floor azimuth indicators were zeroed. The leader then measured the degrees shift found by laying his gun on the target and had all gunners traverse to that reading. He estimated the range and had his, or a better hidden tank, fire bracketing rounds. The elevation for the on-target round was measued with a gunner's quadrant set on the gun breech.

This reading was radioed to the platoon and salvos fired on command. This was a crude but very quick method. The fire director had to correct the range and azimuth if he was not near the platoon.

A extension of this was the use of indirect fire against moving targets. We practiced firing at the moving shadows of clouds in Algeria, on the way up to Tunisia, and in that case the only good distant aiming point we could find was the top of a cloud many miles away. Then, after picking a moving cloud shadow as a target, the leader would measure the distance in mils the shadow moved during the flight of his last ranging shot, lay the platoon on a point ahead of the moving shadow and have the salvo fired when the target came within the determined number of mils. We did use this method once against a group of running troops in Sicily at a range of 4200 yards, with some success, when artillery units were busy with other targets and the platton we used was in a reserve position.

M4s attacking under friendly air burst artillery, a tactic developed in training in French Morocco. An avoidable risk is shown here; combustible equipment was removed if time allowed, before deliberate exposure to shell fire.

Capt. Perkins' sleeping and working area in the Cork Forest of Mamora, French Morocco. This was covered with four standard shelter halves and at night was lighted by an extension cord from the command half-track. Arab grass mats line the wall and floor. Notice the M4 Sherman in the background.

The Man With Big Feet

One of our loaders wore out his size 13-1/2 shoes when we were in Algeria. While waiting for a French factory in Algiers to make him a new pair of shoes, he wore some sandals fashioned from a leather rifle scabbard. This had the happy effect of allowing his air-cooled feet to get rid of a case of athlete's foot but it had the disadvantage of bruised feet when ejected cannon shells landed on them. These empty shells commonly were shoved out through a pistol port in the left rear of the turret but the ordnance people removed the pistol port during four months' production of later tanks, to the anger of tankers

fighting in Europe. Empty .30 caliber shells ordinarily were scooped up by hand, put into empty cannon shells and simply thrown overboard through the hatch.

Training injuries still occurred, even in experienced soldiers. A tank sergeant directed his tank under a tree branch and ducked into his turret. His hands were hooked over the rim of the cupola and all eight fingers were completely severed, sparing only the thumbs, when the branch caught and closed the cupola cover.

Packing for the move to Algeria and Tunisia, May 1, 1943. This officer's impedimenta included a water resistant canvas bedroll and Valpack; shelterhalves; topcoat and rain gear; musette bag for toilet articles (with a shaver which ran slowly on a small 90 volt Signal Corps battery, bug repellent, malaria pills, etc.); steel helmet, helmet liner, tank helmet and field cap; web belt for carrying pistol holster, compass, canvas covered canteen and ammunition clips; a .45 cal. automatic pistol and tommy gun; mess kit; flashlight; whistle; field glasses; message book; rainproof mapcase with crayons, pens, pencils, protractor and ruler; and a foot locker for uniforms, field manuals, other training literature, camera and miscellaneous. Fortunately this could be distributed between tank, halftrack and supply truck.

Tank Compasses

An aircraft compass was mounted near the driver, surrounded by a steel hull and many other strong influences: engine speed, gear changes, hatch covers, rotating turret, guns, stowed equipment, ammunition, metal on crew members, position on the ground and even radios. Compensating the compass required hours of tedious adjustment of magnets, as the tank was turned to compass points marked on the ground. All crewmen and equipment had to be in place, the transmission in neutral, engine running, foot off the clutch, steering levers forward and cannon straight forward. Magnet settings were averaged and deviations recorded for different directions. The compass was not accurate within several degrees and was useful only for giving a general direction, as in woods or at night.

The little GI pocket compasses that we carried on our belts were far more accurate but it was necessary to get out in front of the tank, away from the metal, to take readings. Once in the cork Forest of Mamora, we took a platoon of men on a five-mile hike, plotting every leg of our trip on a map board, using a protractor to record compass measurements on the map. Distances were calculated by counting the same number of paces of ten men in the same rotation for each leg of the hike. After seven or eight changes in direction and detours around obstacles the last and return leg was determined from the map. Miraculously we ended up within ten yards of the starting stake.

On another occasion, periodic dismounted compass readings led our 17 tanks five miles through a cork forest at night, ending within 200 yards of the goal. Another company, depending on the large aircraft compass inside the tank, missed the target by miles.

Maintaining Co. H's kitchen truck, a GMC CCKW-352 2-1/2 tonner.

Supply Problems

An important attribute of a supply sergeant was his willingness not only to beg or borrow, but to steal on occasion, when there was no other provision to fill a need. In Morocco we were required to build shelters for our 75 mm ammunition because the casings were beginning to corrode when stored inside the tank. With no material to make shelters from, my supply sergeant was sent on a mission to find and bring back a pile of lumber. He did so, and we divided it up into 17 equal portions. Each tank crew constructed a little doghouse, copying a model we made. I am afraid a French colonist was the unwitting donor.

On another occasion, on the second day of the invasion of Sicily, we ran out of fuel because of the blowing up of the Liberty Ship *Robert Rowan* by a German dive bomber. We were due to make a big attack the next morning, with just enough fuel to go a few miles at best. Battalion and regimental headquarters had no idea when they would get fuel to us, so I sent First Sergeant Yeo with a 2-1/2 ton truck 25 miles out to the south shore of Sicily to look for some in the middle of the night. He came back

with several hundred gallons, after sneaking it out of a supply dump.

When we went to Sicily we didn't know how much of a breakthrough we were going to be on, whether we were going to be outrunning our supplies, so we had the bottom escape hatches wired shut behind the bow gunner (the assistant driver). With them secured we could pile on them 50 extra rounds of 75 mm, so we carried 140 rounds instead of the regulation 90 and had plenty of ammunition.

Our kitchen truck was a real winner. We had stoves and other kinds of kitchen equipment neatly installed in a 2-1/2 ton truck so that we could cook a complete meal on the road, traveling 40 mph, and serve it in marmite cans. Each marmite can contained a complete hot meal for a tank crew. They would hand the cans out the back of the truck to a jeep and the jeep would hand each can up to a tank commander so we could eat on the move. When we went to Sicily we were ordered to take all of that stuff out in case we had to use the truck for ammunition or fuel.

M4A1 tanks firing from an LCT during invasion training exercises off Port Aux Poules, Algeria. This was in preparation for the invasion of Sicily. (U.S. Army)

Amphibious Action, July, 1943

For the Sicily invasion we had tank engines that had run less than 100 hours since their last periodic overhaul. Spark plugs were supposed to be replaced every 100 hrs on a Wright Whirlwind engine but we pulled all 17 motors anyway, although most only had 50 hrs. We did that in our own bivouac with our own company men just before leaving for Sicily.

On the shore of Lake Bizerte in Tunisia, secretly preparing for our H-hour, D-day beach landing in Sicily, we had 16 tanks and the tank retriever already loaded on five LCTs. The deep wading waterproofing shrouds, already attached, didn't fit very well and we needed more tape and sealing compound. The Quartermaster colonel in charge of the dock refused to give us more. We didn't have time to go through channels so we looked for and found his hidden supply on a truck. I made a rapid raid on it and distributed it to 17 sergeants who ran and hid their shares on the LCT's, while I raced away in my jeep. I narrowly missed being caught by the MPs. My regimental commander, Col. John H. Collier hid me in a tent until dark, then had me taken 10 miles across the lake by motorboat to my LCT, avoiding the dock guards.

The shroud carried air intake and exhaust gasses above the level of the ten-foot high tank. The grill on the top of the rear deck had to be sealed, as did the base of the turret, the pistol port, all gun ports and gun muzzles. We also had to seal all periscopes without blocking the vision. Thus, we could go through nearly ten feet of water. On reaching the shore, rotation of the turret would pull out holding pins by a system of cables on the outside of the tank so as to jettison the shroud. Sometimes the shrouds did not fall off very well and had to be kicked off.

In the Moroccan landings in November 1942

a waterproofed light tank got off a small lighter onto the beach but went in a big circle right back into the ocean and disappeared. The crew may have been asphyxiated by waterproofing sealant vapors or, in any case, couldn't see that they were turning back into the water. Those landings also demonstrated the bad results of landing single tanks from many small landing craft. The boats were swamped or dispersed in rough water. Much better coordination and control came with the use of LCTs (Landing Craft Tank) and LSTs (Landing Ship Tank) which could get pretty close to suitable beaches.

We had had some realistic training for the invasion of Sicily when practicing landings on Tunisian beaches which had not as yet been cleared of German mines. Using our waterproofing shrouds, we were landing from LCTs, 100-foot long landing craft, which could carry three or four medium tanks, with other equipment and troops. My LCT unknowingly was stopped by a sandbar rather than the beach and when we drove my tank down the ramp in the pitch dark we went off into deeper water. I felt the water rise to within a foot of the top of the turret with my fingers, so we were in eight feet of water! I slammed down the turret covers, yelled at the driver to keep going and explained to the crew that if we stalled we would all take a deep breath, open the hatch covers, wait for the water to stop pouring in, and then swim out through the top. We didn't know if we were going into deeper water, so it was a bad scare.

We made it to shore all right, but wire entanglements left by the Germans got caught up in the tracks and kept feeding into them until the tank was stalled. We had to get several wire cutters from other tanks to cut it loose. In the dawn landing in Sicily, July 10, 1943, our LCT crew was so seasick from the stormy night that they failed to open the gates and we had to butt them open with a tank.

The tank crew itself could do quite a lot of repairing. We had a tank track shot up on the first day in Sicily. Some track connectors were broken along one side, a bogey wheel was damaged, and an idler roller was shot off, all by a single armor piercing 75mm round. We managed to move the tank around behind a stone building. Repairs were made with our stowed spare parts while I rode another tank. We then went along all right with one roller gone.

This is an illustration of the single shroud used by M4s during the early dawn, D-Day invasion of Sicily, July 10, 1943. In later amphibious landings, another shroud was added over the engine fan air intake, close behind the turret, to prevent overheating. Notice the cables that pull out holding pins when the turret is rotated after landing. Masking tape had to be manually removed from several places.

Capt. O. Dix Perkins, visiting Signal Corps officer, holds a hand mike in an M4 of the 2nd Armored Division. He helped develop Signal Corps and F.M. tank radios. Capt. Perkins was awarded the Legion of Merit for his pioneering of micro-wave radio relay systems used by him in North Africa and islands in the Mediterranian.

The Radio Net

We had ten different channels by pushbutton for the voice radios and the capability of 100 different channels by changing crystals. Each company had its own assigned channel. We were so well trained before the invasion of Sicily that a crew member in each tank could change and tune the crystals. With the helmet cables plugged in and throat mikes on, crew members could talk to each other, all leaders could talk to all other tanks, and they could change channels to reach other companies or higher echelons.

Tank commanders also had hand microphones for greater clarity and these could be handed out on a long cable for use by someone out of the turret or on the ground. In addition to all the tank radios, we had easily transferred compact SCR 510 transceivers in a jeep and two of the three halftracks.

This is the type of throat microphone used by U.S. Armored Forces in 1943. (U.S. Army)

A Sergeant's Winning Ways

Communications Staff Sergeant Tim McMahan, a tanker by choice, was afraid he would be moved from my tank to the command halftrack or jeep to facilitate his rounds to tanks having radio trouble. So he trained every loader-radio operator to do first echelon radio repairs right in his tank, threatening that he would immediately collect all gambling debts from them and their commanders if they didn't comply. He never had to call the debts.

Not having transistors yet, our radios all had vacuum tubes that often failed with jolting of the tank. McMahan wangled full sets of checked-out replacement tubes from the Signal Corps to be carried in every tank. Since we couldn't quickly tell which tube had been blown we simply changed the whole set, usually correcting a failure in a couple of minutes. The crews vied with each other in speedy repairs.

So McMahan happily was able to stay in the command tank, nursing its radios and declaring that the company would be thrashing around like a dragon with its head cut off if my radio failed. He was right; I couldn't count on jumping into my extra staff tank, because it might be lost as a replacement to one of the platoons. In fact, we had to leave it behind for the Sicily invasion in order to take the T2 tank retriever.

Symbolizing the end in Tunisia, one of the greatest mass surrenders of fully equipped troops in modern history. Clockwise: French helmet; Italian Marines; German Africa Corps; American G.I. and tank helmet with earphones and cable. The German machine gun bolt in the center is an example of the superb craftsmanship of our principal opponent.

Radio Discipline

A tank commander talking to his crew had to be very careful not to let orders unintentionally go out over the radio because it could mislead other crews in the company, all of whom could hear him if he were on radio instead of intercom. Ninety men could hear any radio transmission on the company channel and this included headquarters vehicles, the maintenance section of the company and the communications sergeant in his jeep. This "party line" network demanded good voice discipline and brevity.

During our first battle on the first day in Sicily, one of our platoon sergeants did not recognize the colonel calling me on company channel instead of battalion and said to him, "Listen, you lousy son of a bitch, if you're a goddam Nazi, just keep listening and maybe you'll learn something." We had a good laugh about it as the colonel inspected the six 75 mm guns we had

knocked out.

Our FM radios were supposed to be good only for line-of-sight distance but on one occasion in Tunisia I was able to talk to my company headquarters from fourteen miles away, with a tall mountain intervening. Apparently the radio waves bounced off of something in the stratosphere, perhaps clouds.

Because all leaders required two antennas, we put extra dummy antennas on all other tanks, hoping the enemy could not identify the leaders. However, in my company command tank, I had two transmitters and three receivers. One set was CW for communication with distant higher echelons by Morse code and we needed a third antenna. Because other tanks did not have three, I was picked as a target several times in Sicily before my other tanks were fired on.

Devastated Tiger I near Bizerte, Algeria June 1943. By this stage of the war in North Africa if a German vehicle ran out of fuel or broke down, the quick tide of battle would necessitate the deliberate destruction of the vehicle to prevent it from falling into Allied hands. The absence of tracks and external fixtures suggests this vehicle had been stripped and destroyed by the Germans. Notice the explosion has lifted the turret off of the turret race and repositioned it off center and to the front of the vehicle.

Evacuating A Knocked-Out Tank

One great fear of tankers was of being burned up before they could get out of a tank. Although an entire five-man crew could bail out in five seconds with practice, this is hardly enough time if a penetrating anti-tank or bazooka projectile ignites the propellant in the stored cannon shells, in which case the temperature inside the tank could go to 5,000 degrees within five seconds. So we never locked ourselves into the tank.

On 18 July, 1943, the 2d Armored Division was assembled at Campobello, Sicily, in Seventh U.S. Army reserve, preparing for the drive on Palermo. At that time, the Division was constituted as follows:

Second Armored Division
Commanded by Major General Hugh J. Gaffey

Headquarters and Headquarters Company, 2d Armored Division
Combat Command "A" - Commanded by General Maurice Rose
    Headquarters and Headquarters Company, CC "A"
    66th Armored Regiment
Combat Command "B" - Commanded by Colonel I. D. White
    Headquarters and Headquarters Company, CC "B"
    3rd Battalion, 67th Armored Regiment
41st Armored Infantry Regiment
17th Armored Engineer Battalion (less two companies and H.Q. detachment)
82nd Armored Reconnaissance Battalion (less one company)
Division Artillery
    14th Armored Field Artillery Battalion
    78th Armored Field Artillery Battalion
Companies B and C, 48th Armored Medical Battalion
Detachments from Division Maintenance and Supply Battalion
Attached to the 2d Armored Division were the following:
    1st Ranger Battalion
    4th Ranger Battalion
    106th Coast Artillery Battalion (AA, Self-propelled)
Detachments from 51st Medical Battalion and 36th Ambulance Battalion

Italian Ansaldo 90/53 SP gun M-1941. This vehicle was captured in Sicily and is the same type which knocked out H-17 *Hannibal*, an M4 Sherman. (U.S. Army)

What It's Like To Get Knocked Out

The loss of *Hannibal*, tank H-17/66th in Sicily was an example. We started to fire a smoke shell to mark a distant enemy gun position for our artillery. Our smoke shells had been kept in a bracket on the floor of the turret under the gun breech and must have been stepped on because the one we selected had a dent in the casing. This kept it from seating in the gun chamber and the projectile separated and stuck in the forcing cone. While we were ejecting the shell case and scooping out spilled gunpowder, the gunner misunderstood an order and fired his machine gun. The tracers revealed our position behind concealing foliage, giving the enemy an aiming point and he put a 90 mm armor piercing round through the tree.

The A.P. round, a kind weighing 22.3 lbs, got a freak hit on the muzzle of our cannon.

Otherwise it would have penetrated and possibly killed us all. It tore the cannon loose from its mount, breaking the loader's leg and my (tank commander's) arm. The turret and gun were spun to the left, blocking the driver's escape route through his hatch and through the turret basket. The shot peeled back our gun muzzle like a banana, crashed down into the front slope plate and turned it red hot. The bow gunner got his hot hatch cover open and got out. The driver crawled over the final drive housing and went out the same hatch after another shot took off part of the open hatch cover.

The gunner and I baled out in seconds and the three uninjured men carried the loader away from the tank while still under fire. At that time in the war a common experience was one killed and one wounded per tank knocked out.

An M4 crew prepares their tank for action. Notice the use of tape on the helmet of the crewman handling the hand grenades. Tape was used to hold the headset wires in place. The man receiving the 75 mm shell will discard the tubular case before the shell is passed into the tank for stowage.   (U.S. Army)

The Psychological Preparation For Battle

The 2nd Armored's beloved Maj. Gen. Ernie Harmon, who had left us in Morocco to help straighten out the mess in Tunisia, came back to us briefly in Morocco in early 1943. At an assembly in the cork forest he gave us this philosophy about the possibility of becoming a casualty: "If you are slightly wounded, you're in the gravy...you'll feel like a hero and have a soft touch in the rear echelon for awhile. If you're badly hit, you'll be in shock and not feeling much of anything until you're snapping out of it in a safe place. If you are killed, you won't know it...then what is left? It is the fear of not getting to do all those things back home." Then he said something like, "We're here to see that home will be worth going back to and that we can go back proudly. **Few men are given the privilege that is ours.**"

Epilog

The superb training and indoctrination of the Second Armored Division, which from the beginning considered itself "Patton's own", never allowed it to falter or lose its vibrant esprit de corps and inspired drive. Its spectacular performance earned at least sixteen Distinguished Unit Citations, awarded to infantry, armor, artillery, engineers, reconnaissance and headquarters troops. After 1,702 miles of combat advance, the division was selected, with great honor, as the major unit for occupation of the United States zone in Berlin.

The combat career of the Second Armored Division is beyond the scope of this reminiscence, so only one representative citation will be included here:

Battle Honors, 3rd Battalion, 66th Armored Regiment

As authorized by Executive Order No. 9396 (Sec I, Bull. 22 WD, 1943) superseding Executive Order No., 9075 (Sec III, Bull. 11, WD, 1942) and under provisions of Section IV, Circular No. 333, War Department, 1945, the following unit is cited for extraordinary heroism and outstanding performance of duty in action:

The 3rd Battalion, 66th Armored Regiment, is cited for outstanding performance of duty in action against the enemy during the period 26 July and 1 August 1944, inclusive, in France. For this seven day period the 3rd Battalion constantly spearheaded the advance of Combat Command "A", 2nd Armored Division, which had been assigned the mission of protecting the entire left flank of Operation COBRA. The Battalion boldly and energetically carried the fight to the enemy, pushed deep into the German defensive positions west of the VIRE River, and effectively forestalled enemy attempts to reinforce elements engaged against troops exploiting the breakthrough. From the beginning of the operation the terrain offered almost insurmountable obstacles; sunken roads, thick, high hedgerows and heavy vegetation proved ideal for the defenders and often impassable for armored vehicles. The Battalion overcame every terrain difficulty by energy, resourcefulness and use of field expedients on the part of every tank crew. For seven consecutive days the Battalion was in constant contact with the enemy, advancing 33 miles and inflicting losses on the enemy estimated at twice its own strength in killed, wounded and missing. Its own casualties were extremely heavy: 105% in medium tanks, its greatest striking force; 73% in tank officers and 43% in enlisted personnel of tank crews. Despite these losses, the Battalion carried out every mission it was assigned with the utmost dispatch and vigor. In the last four days of the period, the entire German 2nd Panzer Division was unmercifully mauled and driven back over the VIRE River and the left flank of the breakthrough secured. The success of the operation was due in a large measure to the determination, esprit de corps and cold courage of the officers and men of the 3rd Battalion, 66th Armored Regiment.

Passed by censor for mailing home.

The following article by Staff Sergeant Arden Gatzke in the Milwaukee Journal in 1975 puts the reader back into a tank, which was the original intention of this book:

To me, World War II is a 30 ton tank. A stinky, noisy, crowded, overheated (or freezing cold), bone-shaking iron coffin. For 33 months overseas with the 2nd Armored Division, this tank was my principal home and transportation.

In this tank I watched life and death happen in 10 different countries. I sweated through the heat of Africa and the freezing cold of Belgium during the Battle of the Bulge. I got wet every time it rained.
From this tank aboard an LCT (Landing Craft Tank), I watched as the worst storm in 50 years hit the Mediterranean Sea as we were on our way to invade Sicily. Our little LCT was tossed like a cork, and all but two of us were so seasick we didn't care whether the storm sank the boat or the Germans

did.

From this tank, I watched the fields of Sicily erupt into a sea of white surrender flags as the Italian Army gave up by the hundreds and thousands.

In this tank on June 10, 1944, I rode up onto the beaches of Normandy, France, and again saw the wreckage of war - the dead and dying lying in the fields around Carentan, friend and enemy side by side. The weary paratroopers had been fighting for a week, and they cried as we handed them belts of ammunition. They were down to fighting with bayonets and knives. Their ammunition was gone.

From this tank, I watched the grateful people of France, Belgium and Holland give us flowers and liquor as we liberated their homes from the Germans.

From this tank, I waved goodby to a high school buddy for the last time. We met by chance in a field in France during a three hour lull in battle. Three weeks later, he was dead.

From this tank, I watched an American soldier get up from the ground after an enemy shell exploded next to him. He slung his rifle over his shoulder and walked back to my tank, saying, "The dirty SOBs shot my arm off. Where are the medics?" I pointed to the rear and he just kept on walking, holding onto the stub of his arm.

Near this tank I talked to two little old German women, who were sitting on the steps of their apartment building. They were so glad the Germans retreated from their town, and no shots were fired by either side. The war was nearly over. Then, one last German antitank crew decided to take a shot at my tank. They missed. But the shell hit one of the women and she was blown to bits. The other looked on in disbelief as her own leg rolled down the steps.

Yes, from this tank I watched many events and I still remember...

*　　　*　　　*　　　*　　　*

Our Valhalla waits for us
But we haven't lived enough;
We all live to fight and fight to live
So save a place for us;
If we have to fight to Hell
We won't be back until we're done
And the choice of free men won.

N. H. P. '83

Index